TEACHING YOGA

CREATIVE CUEING FOR SAFER MIXED LEVEL CLASSES

BECCA HEWES

Edited by
ANGELA NICOLOSI

YOGALIFE

Published by Yogalife

Yogalife is a registered trademark of Yogalife, Inc.

Yogalife.tv

Photographs by Alix Yaw

Digital Art by Becca Hewes

Cover Design by Books Covered Ltd.

ISBN 978-1-7347442-0-0 (paperback)

ISBN 978-1-7347442-1-7 (ebook)

Published in the USA

CONTENTS

INTRODUCTION

All of us who choose to teach yoga want to make a positive difference in our students' lives. As our industry and class sizes have grown, our continuing education has become even more important. Many new teachers are asked at gyms and yoga studios to teach large, mixed level classes that even experienced yoga teachers would struggle to teach well. It can be overwhelming when we arrive to teach class and see that it includes a wide variety of people and fitness levels. The increasing popularity of yoga in the last decade has brought everyone we can imagine into our classes. We may find a middle-aged mom, a retired insurance salesman, a former dancer, a college student, and even our own mother all in the same class! What do we do to keep everyone happy and healthy? In my years of teaching yoga, I've faced this situation time and again, and with this book I share the teaching methodology that I've developed to work effectively with the students that attend my classes and trainings. Although I've written this book for new teachers and those attending their first trainings, I believe more experienced teachers may also find some ideas to try in their classes.

My approach to teaching began to develop early on when I became frustrated with how many students came and went from the classes I was teaching at a local gym. Some students did stay, and some have been coming to my classes since I first started teaching, but many students left to pursue some other fitness class within six months. Once I started my own studio, the percentage of people who stayed in classes and became part of the studio community increased, but I still found the average student stayed for less than a year. I realized that if I was going to continue owning a studio, I had to accept that this revolving door was part of the business. Over the years I've had conversations with gym managers, owners of yoga studios, and owners of Pilates studios, who all confirmed experiencing the same thing. As this reality of constant turnover in classes became apparent, I began considering the best way to teach in this environment. What can we best impart to our students in an average of six months that will make the biggest positive impact in their lives? I believe the first skill to introduce is breath awareness. Next, we must focus on basic body awareness to address the modern postural issues created by our electronic devices and sedentary lifestyle. Finally, students need to learn to relax with the practice of Shavasana.

Whether we are teaching yoga or some other physical activity there are movement fundamentals that we can teach to help students become more deeply connected with the body. In order to move efficiently, effectively, and safely, students need to learn these basics. Over time I've developed what I like to call the 10 Yoga Movement Fundamentals. My ideas when creating these fundamentals were influenced by my studies in yoga therapy, my Pilates training with Balanced Body and their Pilates movement principles, and discussions with a number of college-level dance students who attended my trainings. I list the breath first to indicate that it is the most important, and then I start with the feet and move upward for ease of organization of this book.

The 10 Yoga Movement Fundamentals

1. Breath Awareness
2. Opening and Grounding the Feet
3. Aligning the Ankles and Knees
4. Activating the Quadriceps and Glutes
5. Stretching the Hips Carefully
6. Awakening the Core and Stabilizing the Pelvis
7. Freeing the Spine
8. Stabilizing the Shoulders and Opening the Chest
9. Supporting the Wrists, Hands, and Elbows
10. Realigning the Head and Neck

For some students these fundamentals are easy to pick up and execute, but for many they must be practiced again and again. As students begin to gain understanding and strengthen the mind-body connection they will be able to apply a fundamental in one pose, but not necessarily in another. It takes time and patience for students to understand what the teacher is requesting, to have the ability to embody the subtle cues, and to gain the awareness of a deeper yoga practice. However, I believe that if students leave our classes with a better understanding of at least some of these fundamentals, then we've helped them forge a healthier path forward.

I teach these fundamentals through creative cueing and the use of a variety of props. Each chapter in this book covers one of the movement fundamentals in detail, along with cueing ideas, sequencing suggestions, and step-by-step practices for you to explore. The practices in this book are for teachers to try different cues and see what they find. They are for exploration and are not intended for memorization or repeating to students. Most students can only process 3 or 4 verbal cues for each posture at one time. Once students have heard a cue for a while, they will decide that they know what it means (even if they don't) and stop listening. So, to be effective at teaching, we have to vary our cues and change our sequences to keep their attention.

My focus on verbal cueing is intentional. For many years the centerpiece of yoga teacher trainings has been the physical adjustments, with the idea that doing a lot of touching and adjusting is the measure of what makes a great yoga teacher. After learning the common physical adjustments many years ago, I became aware that some students were uncomfortable receiving these adjustments, and in addition some students became overly interested in getting physical adjustments creating boundary issues. Most importantly, I discovered that physical adjustments do not always help the student make their own pose better. To be effective teachers we need more options than just relying on physical adjustments, with a toolbox of both verbal and visual cues.

As our teaching skills grow and develop, our students will learn more quickly how to create their own yoga without depending on us. Being a great yoga teacher is about guiding students to make their own lives a little better through the practice.

1
GUIDING BREATH AWARENESS

Like many yoga teachers, discovering my breath and learning to meditate created a form of awakening, an internal shift within me. This experience was the spark that started my interest in teaching yoga. I wanted to share what I discovered with others. Now as a teacher trainer I hear from students wanting to become yoga teachers, and they all tell me a similar story. Each one of them attempts to put into words some kind of spiritual experience that has occurred, but they don't quite know how to explain it. What they can easily express is that their life is better with yoga, and they want to help others by passing it on.

For many of us, connecting with the rhythm of our breathing and with the accompanying sensations and feelings creates a foundation of awareness that often leads to a spiritual experience. It's that experience that we want to share, that we want so much for others to find. It is what has impelled me to continue to try to teach yoga despite the challenges. But I can't really explain it, and neither can the people calling me on the phone to inquire about teacher training.

I've come to believe that the experience of the breath just happens to people. It's not something that can be controlled or forced. As the teacher I can only create a safe space and situation in which some kind of experience might take place. I am not the doer of this transformation, nor do I take any credit for it. Although I am attempting to teach students about their breath when showing them breathing exercises called pranayama, I consider myself a guide more than a teacher.

A good guide knows the way because they've been there before. They don't talk too much, but they occasionally stop and point things out. Everyone on the tour stops to listen for a few minutes, and then they go on about having their own experience. The guide didn't create the beautiful place and cannot control how great of a tour the participants experience. She can only help them along and see what happens. Some people rate the tour five stars, some give it one star, while others don't even know why they went.

If a student only learns one thing taking my guided tour of yoga, then learning breath awareness is the most important. No matter what we do all day, our breath keeps moving. It's something we can count on to be present throughout life's challenges. The subtle energy of the movement brings comfort and a feeling that we are not alone.

Encouraging Interest in the Breath

With so much to share about our yoga experiences, it can be hard to know where to start when teaching new students breathing. If we take too long with breathing at the start of class, then new students often get bored or anxious, as they are ready for a "workout." On the other hand, if we just jump right into Sun Salutations or other asana, we've missed the chance to introduce them to the breath and to encourage them to remember to breathe throughout class.

At the start of every class, it's helpful to take a moment and have the students sit or lie down to get centered, and then suggest aspects of the breath for them to focus on. It doesn't have to be very long, and in fact with beginners it is often more effective if the centering is short. Here are some examples of cues we might use:

1. Breathe in through the nose and then out through the nose.
2. Feel the cool sensation of the breath coming in at the tip of the nose, and the warmth of the breath on the way out.
3. As you inhale, feel your breath coming in, as you exhale feel your breath coming out.
4. Bring your breath into your ribs and feel the ribs moving.
5. Bring your breath into your chest and feel your chest rising and falling.
6. As you inhale imagine your breath is coming into your abdomen.
7. As you exhale feel the breath coming out of your nose and let your jaw relax.

After we encourage a few minutes or more of centering in silence, the next step is to begin gentle movements connected with the breath. An example would be the common cue, "inhale as you lift your arms, exhale as you bring them down."

DEEPENING THE UNDERSTANDING OF THE BREATH AND OUR HEALTH

At some point in our youth many of us were told by a coach or choir director to "breathe from your diaphragm." I remember hearing this instruction in high school and having no idea what it meant. Until I took anatomy later on in school, I didn't even know where my diaphragm was located. Because of this experience I choose not to use the word "diaphragm" in my mixed level classes, and instead focus on imagery to help students breathe more freely and in a relaxed manner. As teachers though, we need to understand the basics of how breathing works, and the different ways in which to breathe.

The diaphragm is considered the primary muscle for breathing as it moves our rib cage; it also works continually in the background. The scalene and sternocleidomastoid muscles in the neck assist the diaphragm when needed by helping to lift the rib cage and are considered accessory (secondary) muscles of respiration. When the diaphragm struggles to move enough breath, then the accessory muscles join in to help. The need for the accessory muscles occurs during exercise, colds, allergies, and other times when our ability to breathe is challenged. Accessory breathing muscles are not meant to be used for this purpose all the time as they have other main functions, and when overused to lift the rib cage they can cause pain and headaches. Other muscles that attach to the rib cage are also considered accessory breathing muscles, such as the pectoralis major and minor, serratus anterior, upper trapezius, and levator scapula.

When we heard the instruction "breathe from your diaphragm," most likely the teacher was cueing us to take deep belly or abdominal breaths. What we have learned though is that many students struggle to learn abdominal breathing. Sometimes this is because they hold a lot of tension in the belly, and so they have a pattern of breathing into their chests. Most new yoga students are unaware of their breathing patterns and may not have given it much thought. One lesson we need to review again and again is the difference between abdominal breathing, chest (clavicular) breathing, and rib cage breathing.

Abdominal breathing is a relaxed breath, it is not about using the abdominals to push the stomach in and out. In this natural breath, the belly begins to move outward because the viscera (your organs and fluid around them) of the lower abdominal cavity are compressed as the lungs fill with air. The downward compression causes the belly to stick out. On the exhale the pressure is relieved, and the belly moves inward. The ribs also gently move in this natural and healthy breathing pattern.

Stretching and relaxing the abdominals can be helpful to encourage students to "belly breathe" but it can take time and sometimes different cues and imagery for them to understand. Focusing on the belly while breathing, without cueing students to take any muscular action, is a nice start. Although I and many other teachers have used the common cue, "breathe into your belly" for years, for some students it doesn't make much more sense than "breathe from your diaphragm." One creative cue that works for me and some of my students who do well with imagery comes from a vocal teacher Nancy Zi. In her book *The Art of Breathing,* she describes abdominal breathing in this way, "Imagine yourself to be an upside-down eyedropper. Squeeze the bulb, and air is squeezed out. Release the bulb, letting it expand, and air is drawn into the body."[1] In this image we imagine that the bulb of the eye dropper is in our abdomen and the tip of the dropper is up behind our nose. The lesson is that there is no effort for the breath to come in when the bulb is released.

In chest breathing (clavicular breathing), the abdominals move in on the inhalation and the chest and collarbones lift. This shallow form of breathing overuses the accessory muscles and may cause long term health issues. People who chest breathe often take shorter "sips" of breath and may also have a pattern of breath holding. Yoga therapists continue to note how unhealthy breathing patterns such as chest breathing may be at the heart of some undiagnosed medical problems. However, the medical community for the most part has not yet embraced this idea. Some medical practitioners are beginning to investigate these observations though and have coined the term breathing pattern disorder (BPD).[2]

In healthy breathing we see easy, relaxed movement in the whole torso, including movement in the back and side body. The 360-degree breathing must also include a gentle consistent cadence without a lot of movement in the neck. Donna Farhi in her work, *The Breathing Book,* describes this cadence as "calm and regular" in her detailed discussion of "free and effective breathing."[3] Learning a relaxed and easy cadence is a great first step for new students.

Let's take a moment to practice breathing into different parts of our torso, including our rib cage, which we will discuss in depth below as it relates to active asana.

Practice: Breathing into the Abdomen, Ribs, Chest, and Back

1. Lie on your back with your feet flat and your knees up. If needed, place a bolster under your knees for comfort.
2. After you settle in and get comfortable, bring your attention to your breath.
3. Notice if your belly, your ribs, and/or your chest move as you breathe in and out. Does one area move more than another?
4. Place your hands on your belly and as you breathe notice if you feel the belly rise and fall. Come into a nice easy breath. Notice that your ribs may not move as much when you are focusing on the belly.
5. Place your hands onto your chest, again letting the elbows rest at your sides, with support if needed. Bring your breath into your chest, feeling it rise and fall.
6. Next place your hands on your ribs while continuing to let your elbows rest on the floor. Bring your breath into the ribs, and feel the ribs expand with the inhale and soften on the exhale. Notice how the belly may be quieter now while you are focusing on the ribs.
7. Let your arms lie comfortably by your sides and focus on your back ribs. As you inhale, see if you can feel some movement of the ribs on the mat.
8. Take a big 360-degree breath into the ribs and see how far you can expand in all directions.
9. Finish with some quiet natural breaths.

BREATHING IN ACTIVE ASANA

This basic awareness of our breathing is a very important first step when doing active asana. If a student has a pattern of holding the breath — breathing more into one area such as the chest, or never taking a deep inhale — then they will struggle more than other students when the asana becomes challenging. As they become more aware of their breathing, we can teach them active rib breathing. This type of breathing is cued in various ways depending on the exercise tradition. Some yoga teachers call this type of breathing side breathing or lateral rib breathing. I have heard Pilates teachers asking their students to "breathe wide to the side" as they were doing core work.

With beginning students, I introduce this concept by having them sit comfortably and put their hands on their ribs. I then ask them to bring as much breath into their ribs as they can. Students can feel the ribs moving and the thoracic cage expanding. As we sit and breathe into our ribs they move upward like the handle of a bucket.[4] I will also encourage students to firm their bellies gently as they are practicing this rib breathing.

Why is rib breathing important? When we are in challenging postures our core needs to be working, not relaxed, or we will lack stability and endurance. If students are breathing into their abdomens with a relaxed core rather than their ribs, then they will either be less stable, or they will be using their large surface muscles to try and stabilize themselves without core integration. We will dive deeper into the topic of core integration in Chapter 6.

Working with a simple standing pose like Tree is a great way to teach students how breathing into their ribs allows them to keep their core engaged and their pelvis stable during active asana. Then we can encourage them to apply this movement fundamental in many of the active postures.

Practice: Rib Breathing in Tree

1. Place your mat near a wall, stand with your right side next to the wall and come into Mountain. Place your hands on your ribs. As you inhale, feel your ribs moving with your breath.
2. Lift your low belly in and up, keeping your core engaged as you continue to feel your ribs moving.
3. Place your right hand on the wall and your left hand on your

hip. Spread your toes, lift your arches, and then begin shifting your weight onto your right foot.

4. Keep your right hip in a neutral position and your right knee tracking in line with your toes. If your knee is not tracking with your toes and starting to point medially (inward), then ever so slightly turn your hip out letting your knees and toes follow.
5. Bring your left foot up and place it on your right leg either below your knee on the inner calf or above your knee on the inner thigh. Press your left foot into your right leg and press your leg back into your foot.
6. Without forcing your left knee to the side, let your left knee move out to the left as far as it can without any pinching in your hip, or your back beginning to arch.
7. Check in with your core again and firm your lower belly by drawing it in and up. Imagine your front hip pointers (anterior superior iliac spine, or ASIS) are drawing towards each other as you feel your deep inner core engage.
8. Firm your glutes by grounding your sit bones towards your heels.
9. Keeping this firm foundation you've created from your pelvis to the floor, begin to elongate your spine upward as if you are reaching through the crown of your head. Imagine you are trying to lift your ribs upward away from your pelvis.
10. If you feel your back beginning to arch and your ribs popping forward, then firm your upper abdominals to draw your lower ribs inward. Imagine you are connecting the front of your lowest ribs to your hip pointers.
11. Keep your shoulders relaxed in a comfortable neutral position, neither holding them up towards the ears nor actively forcing them down.
12. Feel your shoulder blades gently firming on your back, as you let the collar bones widen.
13. Let your jaw and face relax and feel the breath coming in and out of the nose.

14. While keeping your core stable, continue breathing into your ribs. Take a moment to bring your left hand up to your ribs and feel them moving. If you struggle with balancing, then keep your right hand on the wall.
15. If you feel balanced, then bring your hands to your heart. Gently press your hands together or stretch them up over your head.
16. To come out of the pose, place your hands on your hips and bring your left foot back to your mat. Take a few breaths in Mountain.

BALANCING THE CADENCE AND DEPTH OF THE BREATH WITH UJJAYI

Once students begin to notice and connect with their breath, we can also encourage them to notice the cadence or pattern of their breathing. Are inhales almost as long as exhales? Are the breaths long and smooth, or short and constricted? One foundational practice that teaches smooth, even breathing is Ujjayi. In this common pranayama technique, the practitioner makes a gentle sound in their throat as the breath comes in and out. In some forms of yoga, students are told to breathe loudly so that the teacher can hear it. In other forms, students are asked to make just enough sound to hear it themselves and maybe the person practicing next to them.

Whatever volume students pick for their Ujjayi, the idea is to create smooth, long, steady breathing throughout their practice. This must be done with a relaxed throat and jaw, so if trying to make a louder sound is creating tension in the jaw, then it is better to focus on the smoothness and cadence rather than the volume. Once they have learned this foundational breathing exercise, students can then begin to learn other pranayama techniques to help them settle into relaxation. See more on this subject in Chapter 11.

Practice: Beginning Ujjayi

1. Sit comfortably and bring your attention to your breathing.
2. Breathe in and out of the nose slowly, steadily taking the time to exhale as long as you inhale.
3. Keeping your mouth closed, imagine that you are saying "haaaaa" on the exhalation and listen for the change in the sound of your breath.[5]
4. Continue to try to make a gentle sound like this on both the exhale and the inhale, focusing the sound in your throat and not your sinuses.
5. Keep the volume low like a whisper, and the breath steady like soft waves coming in and out.

TRADITIONAL YOGA BREATHING WITH SPECIFIC MOVEMENTS

Although any focus on the breath is positive, there are some traditional breathing cues for specific movements.

- When we move into forward bends the tradition is to exhale. As we move into a seated forward bend such as Head to Knee, we exhale. Once in the forward bend we inhale to lengthen the spine and then exhale as we move deeper.
- When we move into a backbend the tradition is to inhale. As we move into Cobra we inhale. Once in the posture we breathe slowly and consistently deepening the backbend on the inhales and lengthening on the exhales.
- When we move into twists the tradition is to exhale. As we move into the seated twist, Half Lord of the Fishes, we exhale. Once in the twist we inhale to lengthen the spine, and then exhale to deepen the twist.

These traditions have endured because they feel good and they work, but it is fine to experiment and breathe in different ways in the postures. I deviate from these traditional breathing cues in my own practice and teaching where a significant exertion will occur. Our core, specifically the transverse abdominals and the muscles that work with them, activate better on the exhalation. An activated deep core helps to support and protect the body from injury and keeps the large surface muscles from taking over and dominating the pose. For example, when I press up into Wheel, a full backbend pose, I press up on an exhalation even though the tradition is the opposite. The exhale helps me stay integrated in my core and protects my back as I lift up. Once I'm in the pose then I move into the traditional breathing, inhaling to subtly deepen the backbend, and then activating my core during the exhale while lengthening my lower back.

Examples of Traditional Breathing in Asana

Cat/Cow, where we roll through the spine while on the hands and knees, has become a staple of modern classes. It didn't appear in many of the first American yoga books and seems to have been added to the practice as yoga and fitness began to merge.[6] The Cat/Cow movement is a great warm-up for the spine and the abdominals, but the rounded thoracic spine of the deep Cat position isn't really where most modern students need to focus. Many of us are already walking around with our shoulders and thoracic spines rounded over. One option when teaching Cat is to cue students to take the time to gently work in the lumbar spine first, instead of moving too quickly into the upper thoracic. As students move into Cow pose, we need to cue the core and encourage slowing down to keep them from overextending and hanging in their lumbar spines. Although Cat/Cow is easy for most of us and is used as a gentle warm-up, older students with low back and posture issues may not get much benefit from it, and even risk hurting themselves if they go too deeply too quickly. So when teaching mixed groups, after a few Cat/Cow repetitions to help students connect to the breath, it's good to move on into variations of the Opposite Arm/Leg Balances on the hands and knees. These variations, sometimes called Bird Dog or Sun Dog by different teachers, help to strengthen the low back and core and often reduce everyday back pain. See Chapter 6 for more on this topic.

Practice: Traditional Breathing in Cat/Cow

1. Come onto your hands and knees. Bring your hands slightly forward of your shoulders, shoulder-width apart, and your knees under your hips, hip-distance apart.
2. If kneeling on the mat is uncomfortable, try placing a blanket down first.
3. Widen through your chest and gently firm your shoulder blades onto your back.
4. Lengthen through the crown of your head in one direction and your pelvis in the opposite direction, elongating your spine.
5. Keep your neck in line with your spine. Avoid lifting the head up or letting it hang down.
6. Take an inhale to prepare, and then as you exhale start by drawing your low belly in and up.
7. Isometrically press your hands gently away from your knees to help activate your core as you begin to move into Cat. Imagine your hip pointers are drawing towards each other as you round your back.
8. Feel your pubic bone begin to reach up towards your belly button, as you gently round the lower back.
9. Take your time going vertebrae by vertebrae through your low back first, then moving into your middle and upper back as you move into the full Cat position.
10. At the end of the exhalation, pause for a moment to enjoy the stretch of the full Cat pose.
11. As you begin inhaling, start the movement at the base of your spine again, slowly letting your low back begin to arch, moving one vertebra at a time.
12. Isometrically press your hands gently towards your knees to

help draw your heart forward, bringing the backbend into your upper back.

13. Let your heart lead you into Cow while letting the neck and head follow to avoid sending your neck into a deep extension.
14. At the end of the inhalation, pause for a moment to enjoy the stretch of the full Cow pose.
15. Take your time gently going between Cat/Cow following the rhythm of your breath.
16. To come out of the pose, sit back into Child's pose and breathe.

For our second example of traditional breathing, let's look at the seated Sage Twist. In this pose, the tradition is to inhale as we lengthen the spine and exhale as we twist. The main challenge when teaching this pose is to encourage students to engage their core and move their ribs, rather than forcing themselves around with their arms and shoulders.

When students crank themselves around, they risk injuring their low back, sacroiliac (SI) joints, and shoulders. The thoracic spine, especially around vertebrae T11/T12, is designed to twist much more so than the lumbar spine, so our focus needs to be on a strong core engagement and stability in the pelvis, and then movement of the rib cage. Although the upper cervical spine is built for quick rotation, the best practice is to cue students to lead the twist with their abdominals and rib cage and let the head and neck follow.

When we move into a twist from the head and eyes, this often creates tension and a feeling of being stuck in the back of the upper neck. Abdominal breathing can be used as a starting point to get grounded on the mat, but once we begin cueing students into the pose, it's better to change to rib breathing. Rib breathing allows for a deeper rotation while the core remains engaged.

In this gentler version of Sage Twist, students use the fingertips to support the upper body and activate the core. The focus is on rotating through the ribs rather than a deep cervical twist.

Practice: Traditional Breathing in Sage Twist

1. Start sitting in Staff pose with your legs long in front of you and your fingertips on the floor at your sides. If your fingers do not touch the floor, place blocks under your hands.
2. If you have trouble sitting up straight, sit on a folded blanket.
3. Bring the feet about hip-distance apart. Bend the right knee and place the right foot on the mat. How much you bend your knee depends on your comfort level and range of motion.
4. As you inhale, sit as tall as you can and lengthen your spine. Draw your belly in and up to help support you. Press into your fingertips for support.
5. Firm your left thigh and ground your left heel, keeping the left knees and toes pointing straight up.
6. On your next exhale, begin twisting your ribs to the right

while focusing on moving your ribs with your abdominal muscles. Keep your fingers planted at first.

7. As you twist towards your right, engage your low belly, below your belly button, towards the left. If your left hip naturally twists a little to the right following your ribs, then let it.
8. Place your left hand on your right shin or around your right knee, and place your right fingertips to your side and slightly behind you with your fingertips pointing toward your feet.
9. Once you've twisted as far as you can with your abdominals, begin to carefully add a little extra rotation with your hands and shoulders. Gently press your right fingertips isometrically into the mat and forward toward your feet while feeling your right shoulder blade firm onto your back.
10. Press your left hand into the right side of your right leg. Press your right leg back into your left hand.
11. Exhale as you deepen the twist. Inhale as you lengthen your spine.
12. Turn your neck to the right as is comfortable. There is no need to force the neck to look behind you.
13. To leave the pose, continue to keep your core engaged and bring your hands to the floor for support as you come out of the rotation and stretch your right leg out. When you feel ready, switch legs and repeat on the other side.

SUBTLE BREATHING EXPERIENCES FOCUSING ON ONE SIDE

As students begin to build awareness of their breath, they can move into more subtle experiences. Sometimes a very small change in breathing can make a huge difference in how the pose feels. One example is trying to breathe more into one lung than the other. When I first suggested this to a group of students recently, I was met with resistance. One student exclaimed, "You can't do that!" I gently responded that indeed I can do it and over time I have even increased the volume I can take into one side at a time. This technique can be used in twisting asanas to gently deepen the rotation. It can also be used in a pose with side flexion to assist opening up the stretched side with the breath. In every pose there is an opportunity to deepen the experience with the breath in some way.

Practice: Breathing into One Lung More than the Other

1. Sit in a comfortable position on the floor or a chair.
2. Place your hands on your ribs, wrapping your thumbs around toward your back.
3. As you inhale through your nose, focus your attention on your right lung and ribs.
4. Imagine you are breathing entirely into your right lung and ribs.
5. It may take some time and focus until you feel any sensation – but if you work at it you may begin to feel the right side moving more than your left.
6. Now focus on your left side, imagining that you are breathing more into your left lung and ribs. Notice if the sensations you feel are the same or different from your right side.
7. Return to your natural relaxed breathing into both lungs.
8. If you didn't feel anything this time, then just be patient, keep breathing, and try again later.

SUBTLE BREATHING EXPERIENCES FOCUSING BEHIND THE HEART

Learning to breathe in different ways helps us to discover if we are not breathing into certain areas of our lungs. Having healthy lungs is so important to our overall health that I practice breathing into all areas of my lungs each day. It doesn't take too long, and I always feel better when I'm done. One area I enjoyed discovering is the lung tissue behind the heart.[7] The heart makes an imprint on the left lung, and there is also a groove for the aorta. The area between the shoulder blades is often tight, and the spine has less movement there than in other areas. It is designed that way to protect the heart. Students often feel a tightness or mild discomfort when they first access and focus on this part of the lungs. This breathing can be helpful in asanas like Downward Dog and Dolphin where students often get locked up in their rhomboids and upper trapezius muscles. For more on this topic, see Chapter 8.

Practice: Breathe Behind your Heart

1. Sit comfortably on your mat and bring your attention to your breath.
2. After a few relaxed breaths, bring your attention to the area between your shoulder blades and try imagining you are breathing into that area. It can often be found toward the end of the inhalation, rising up the spine first and then expanding outward between the shoulder blades.
3. You may even feel like the shoulder blades are moving apart as the upper back widens.
4. Stay with it for a few breaths to connect and deepen the experience.
5. Once you think you've found it, try coming into your Downward Dog and try it again. Feel your upper back widen and your underarms hollow out.

Daily Practice + Breath Awareness

Most students come to yoga having paid little attention to their breath or the cadence of it. Their breath has continued behind the scenes going unnoticed. When they finally slow down and pay attention, this sometimes creates tension. They may try to control the breath too much with forced inhales and exhales. After they give up trying to control the breath, they fall back into their natural breathing pattern. Through simple breathing exercises and reminders, we are guiding them to find a daily awareness of their breath that over time centers them and encourages healthier breathing patterns. In every class we teach we need to remind students to breathe at least a few times during class, especially during more strenuous asanas. Every week someone comes up to me after class and thanks me for reminding them to breathe. I often hear, "I didn't realize I was holding my breath!"

2

OPENING AND GROUNDING THE FEET

The health of our feet reflects the health of our body. If our feet are tight and painful, then it is likely that other areas of our body are also tight and painful. We depend on our feet to get us around, so it's worth the time to pay attention and take care of them. Foot care is more than a pedicure; it's about stretching and strengthening all the little muscles of the feet. Many of us spend the majority of our day in shoes where our toes and arches don't get a chance to stretch or work properly.

When new students come to yoga and we ask them to take off their shoes, we have a great opportunity to teach them the importance of foot care and awareness. For some new students, taking off their shoes makes them uncomfortable. They need encouragement and acceptance as they are embarrassed by the way their feet look. Other students have no issue taking off their shoes but haven't given any attention or thought to their feet at all. By introducing toe exercises and the use of balls to massage our arches during class, we can begin to guide students toward an awareness of their feet.

Practice: Fancy Toe Yoga

1. Sit on your mat with your knees up and your feet flat on the mat.
2. If you can't easily see your toes in this position, then sit up on some blankets or blocks.
3. Keeping your feet on the floor, try to lift all your toes up and spread them out.
4. See how far apart you can stretch your toes. If two toes don't want to separate, reach down with your fingers and work gently to separate them.
5. Notice which toes may not want to lift up much and which ones don't want to spread out.
6. Bring them down and wiggle them to relax.
7. Lift all the toes up again, and see if you can put just the big toes down while keeping all the other toes up.
8. Next, use your hands to hold down all your toes except your big toes. Then try lifting both of your big toes up and then towards each other to work the muscles on the medial side of your feet.
9. Bring your big toes down, and again take a moment to relax and wiggle all the toes.
10. The next step is to focus on your little toes. Start by lifting up all the toes, keeping the rest of the foot grounded on the mat. Stretch the pinky toe out and place it on your mat, while still trying to keep all the other toes lifted up.
11. Slowly begin to move one toe at a time to the floor until all the toes are on the floor again.
12. Finally lift up all the toes, including your big toes, and spread them out. Try moving your big toes and your pinky toes to the mat while leaving your three middle toes up.
13. Finish by relaxing and massaging your feet.[1]

Opening the Feet

These toe exercises usually spark some giggling, which is a good thing. As students are working on these exercises, they get so focused on their toes that they don't notice their hands and fingers getting curled and tense trying to help. When I bring it to their attention they usually start laughing even more. But through all the giggles students become more aware of their feet and improve their balance while stretching and strengthening the toes.

For students who have toes that don't move or spread out well, I recommend they visit a beauty supply store and buy some toe separators that are used for pedicures. Placing the toe separators in between the toes while watching TV or reading at night can help to start opening up the foot. Spreading, flexing, and extending the toes with the toe separators in is also helpful. Once the brain and the toes reconnect, these students are often able to stretch out the toes again without the separators. Cramping is an issue, especially for those people who haven't been working with their feet much. In these cases, a little goes a long way; start slowly to build strength and tolerance, maybe working just one foot at a time.

Tight feet often reflect tight legs, hips, and low backs. With some students, working on the feet with tennis balls or other small rubber balls can bring relief from tightness and tension in these areas. Instruct students to roll their feet out on the balls towards the beginning of class. If they can tolerate it, encourage them to add some body weight on the foot with the ball underneath the arch. Some yoga and Pilates studios have a tradition of students coming in and getting a ball to work on their feet before class even starts.

WORKING WITH THE FEET IN STANDING POSES

Yoga teachers often will use language such as "ground through the feet" or "root the feet." Although I love this imagery, it doesn't always connect with every student. Another popular cue, is to "ground through the four corners of the feet." The four corners of the feet include the big toe mound, the little toe mound, and the inner and outer heel. All of these cues are attempting to communicate the same thing: that the weight should be distributed evenly throughout the foot. In my own teaching I have settled on simplifying the cue for beginners by saying, "ground into your big toe mounds and your outer heels." With this simple cue, I'm asking the students to bring equal weight to the front and the back of their feet, while also distributing their weight equally to both the inside and outside of their feet.

Our feet are our foundation in the standing poses. How we place them and engage them affects our alignment throughout the body, and in turn our balance. Mountain is a great basic position to introduce students to grounding the feet and feeling energy drawing in and upward. The practice below is a beginning summary for students. These basic alignment fundamentals in Mountain apply to all our standing postures, and we will work through them in the upcoming chapters.

Practice: Mountain

1. Standing with your feet hip-distance apart, lift and spread your toes out and put them back down.
2. Press into your big toe mounds and your outer heels evenly.
3. As you ground through your big toe mounds and outer heels, lift your toes again and feel your arches lift. See if you can keep that feeling of being engaged and lifted arches as you put the toes back down.
4. Imagine the energy from your arches rising into your legs, and firm your thighs and feel your kneecaps lift up.
5. Draw your low belly in and up to feel your abdominals and pelvic floor lift.
6. Try to find a neutral place for your pelvis with a natural lumbar curve, where your low back is neither too straight nor too arched.
7. Keeping your pelvis stable, bring your attention to your ribs

and notice if they have moved forward creating an arch in your middle back. If so, then draw your upper abs (just below the ribs) in and up and bring your front ribs inward so that you are not in a backbend. Imagine your lowest ribs are connected to your hip pointers.

8. Let your shoulders relax down and away from your ears, without actively forcing them down and creating tension.
9. Imagine you are widening your collar bones away from each other as the shoulders move back and down.
10. Lengthen the back of your neck upwards and reach through the crown of your head.
11. See if you can experience the energetic connections from your feet to the top of your head.

COMMON CUES THAT CONFUSE SOME NEW STUDENTS

Over the years I've witnessed many students who have had trouble understanding basic movement instruction including where to place their feet. Sometimes this is due to a lack of movement class experience or from never being involved in sports, but people can become disconnected from their bodies for a wide variety of reasons. These students are sometimes confused when they hear the common cue "widen your stance" or "lengthen your stance." They look around the room at the other students, and then they move their feet in the opposite direction than we intended! For example, in Warrior 1, we might cue the student to widen their feet apart, but instead they take a bigger step back. "Widening" is generally used to describe moving our feet out to the sides away from the midline. "Lengthening" a stance usually describes taking one foot in front of you while the other foot goes behind you. The problem builds when students are asked to move around and face different directions on their mats. They become disoriented, and the terms quickly become ineffective.

I still use "widen" and "lengthen" in my teaching, but I try to use a few other options when I see students are struggling. The first and often best option is to move in front of them and demonstrate the stance. If they are visual learners, then they will quickly figure it out. The second option is to try a very specific verbal cue such as, "try moving your left foot towards the back of the room." Simply slowing down the pace of the class is another effective solution.

Other common terms that are used by yoga teachers to describe positions on the mat can also be confusing to inexperienced students. For instance, if we walk up to one of the shorter edges of the mat and stand in Mountain, I refer to the way we are facing as the "front of the mat." Some instructors refer to this position as the "top of the mat." It is also common to refer to the "front leg" or "back leg" in a posture. For most people it is clear which is the front and back leg, but some students will get confused in poses like Triangle where we are facing the long side of the mat. For these students I will explain that the "front" leg in Triangle is the one closest to the "front" of the mat where we started in Mountain.

VARIATIONS IN STANCES FOR THE STANDING POSES

How do we determine the best stance for each student? We want students to separate their feet enough to feel challenged, but still be able to ground through their big toe mounds and outer heels to stay balanced and stable. In addition, they should feel no pain, pinching, or compression in their hip and knee joints. Let students start where they feel comfortable and set their own pace for going deeper.

Each style of yoga may offer its own variations of stances for the standing postures. An example would be in Warrior 1, where some teachers will ask students to take a very big step back, while others might ask them to take a comfortable step back. The farther the step back, the more athletically challenging the pose will be, but the harder it will be for students to ground into their outer heels and activate the glutes.

In some traditions, students are asked in Warrior 1 and Warrior 2 to take a stance where their front thigh is parallel to the floor. This flexes the hip at 90-degrees and is a great workout for the thighs, but many students cannot maintain poses this deep without losing their balance or feeling discomfort in their joints.

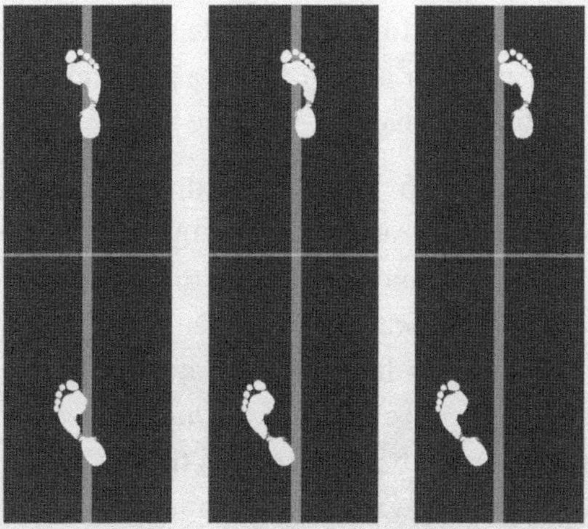

Although the traditional heel-to-arch alignment on the left works for some, many women feel better with the heel-to-heel placement in the center. For others the slightly wider stance on the right works best.

We can learn to engage our muscles to create the challenge rather than rely on extreme range of motion. In my own practice, I've found it helpful to vary my stances in the standing poses because it works the muscles of the legs and hips in different ways.

Traditionally in standing poses like Warrior 1, Triangle, and Side Angle the foot placement has been cued "heel to arch" with the front heel in line with the arch of the back foot. There are some students who feel great in the heel to arch stance, but they tend to be those with narrow hips. When modern yoga asana was popularized in India in the 1920's, many of the students were young men who could stand heel to arch with no issues[2]. Women have naturally wider pelvises, which includes a greater Q angle of the femur.[3] This puts pressure on the hip joints and the knees when the stances are practiced with the heel to arch placement. Although this alignment continues to be taught in many yoga communities, there are other options that are more accessible and easier on the joints for many students. For some time now, I've been practicing and teaching the Warrior poses and other standing poses heel to heel or a little wider. In some cases, with those clients who are older or have balance problems, I will have them place the feet even wider than hip-distance apart.

If we encourage students to focus on stability first, then most of them will naturally find the best stances for themselves. For those who struggle and need more guidance, I'll ask them to imagine a yoga mat with a line drawn all the way down the length of the mat in the very center. I call this the long line. Then I ask them to imagine another line drawn across the entire width of the mat in the very center. I call this the short line. Once they understand this image, I can easily cue them to "move your feet away from the short line," or "move your feet closer to the long line." This imagery is particularly effective when helping students with the heel-to-arch or heel-to-heel option discussed above. For example: to help them find their best foot placement in Pyramid, ask them to imagine the long line down the middle of their mat as a thick line. Ask them to try three different placements for their feet. First place their feet with one arch and the other heel on the line (the traditional heel-to-arch stance), then with both heels on the line, and finally place the heels to either side of the line. Ask them to notice which options make them feel the most stable without any pinching, pain, or compression in their joints.

Practice: Pyramid

1. Starting in Mountain, place two blocks in front of you about shoulder-width apart. Then returning to Mountain, take a comfortable step back with your right foot. Place your heels in a line or a little wider, whichever is most comfortable for you.

2. Turn your right hip out by pivoting on your right big toe mound, letting your knee and toes follow the hip turn-out.
3. Ground through your big toe mounds and outer heels, bringing equal weight into both feet.
4. Feel your arches lift and energize, and then bring that energy from your feet up into your legs and hips.
5. Engage your thighs and your glutes as you continue to connect your feet to the mat.
6. From this grounded and firm position, inhale as you lengthen your spine up, reaching through the crown of your head.
7. Shift your pelvis a little bit to your right, encouraging the grounding of your right outer heel into the mat.
8. "Zip up" your belly from pubic bone to belly button, by drawing your low belly in and up.
9. Place your hands on your hips. While keeping an elongated spine, start to fold forward at the hips and bring your torso over your left leg.
10. Resist the urge to round your spine as you fold forward, and instead work on keeping your spine elongated.
11. When your pelvis cannot fold any farther forward, stop there and either leave your hands on your hips, or if you are low enough place your hands onto your blocks. Adjust the blocks so they are under your shoulders.
12. Imagine you are lifting the crown of the head again, elongating your spine while keeping your low belly toned.
13. To more deeply engage your thighs and glutes, imagine you have a resistance band around your thighs, and you are working your thighs and feet away from the long line down the middle of your mat. (In other words, imagine you are moving your left leg to the left and your right leg to the right. This is called abduction of the hips.)
14. To gently deepen the stretch on the left hamstrings, twist your ribs slightly to the left and bring your torso a little more over your left leg.
15. Breathe into your ribs while toning your low belly.

16. To come out of the pose, bring your torso to the center and then soften your knees and imagine you are pressing your legs away from each other as you come up.

WORKING WITH ACTIVE FEET IN ALL POSES

In this chapter, we've focused on grounding our feet into the mat in standing poses. Now let's talk about keeping our feet active in one-legged standing poses like Warrior 3 and Half Moon where one foot is not weight bearing. These are popular poses on social media where we can see the various foot positions students choose, including flexed, pointed, somewhere in-between, and even floppy, unengaged feet.

When the foot is not weight-bearing, traditional hatha yoga teachers prefer a gently flexed foot with the toes extended (lifted). This foot position has different names depending on the yoga community. Some teachers call it "yoga toes" while others like to joke around and call it "Barbie feet." Some have even used the term "flointing" to express that the position is somewhere between pointing and flexing.

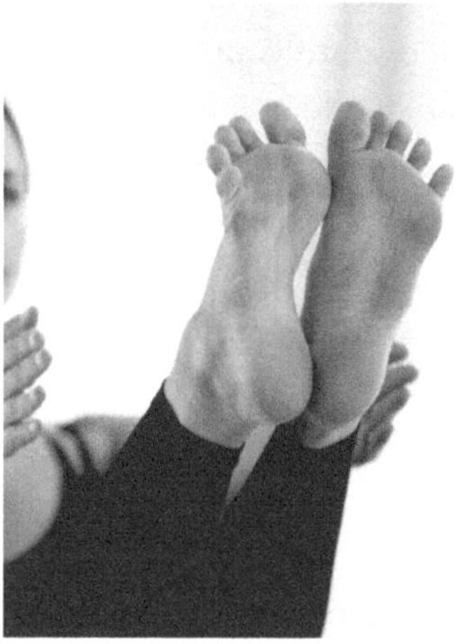

Keeping the feet active helps to bring energy into the legs, hips, and core. To create "yoga toes" the feet are somewhere between pointed and flexed with arches engaged and toes spread.

The idea behind the "yoga toes" position is both to awaken the arches and work the muscles evenly on each side of the legs. When our leg is up in the air behind us in Warrior 3, we want all of our muscles engaged to help lift and stabilize the pose. Pointing the foot activates the muscles on the back of the calf, while flexing activates the muscles on the front of the shin. When we add a little of both actions, we achieve a deeper and more even muscle engagement. This position can be overdone, with some teachers insisting on an extreme toe extension or ankle flexion that creates tension in the feet and lower legs over time. For the majority of students, it is better to focus on gently engaging the feet. A little foot work goes a long way in awakening the arches and energizing the legs.

This "yoga toes" position is also used in many of the seated poses. Engaging the feet and legs while we are stretching helps to focus the stretch on the muscles rather than the joints, which is especially important for our more flexible students. I activate my feet in this way in all of the seated poses, feeling the energy coming up from my arches all the way into my hips.

Options for Staff

This is a great seated pose to try the different positions for your feet and ankles and to see how your foot position affects how the pose feels energetically.

Although at first glance Staff may seem like a simple and easy pose, the reality is that many people need to modify the posture due to tight hips, hamstrings, and backs. For these students, placement of the pelvis up higher than the thighs reduces the angle of the hips and gives the hamstrings some relief. One option is to have them sit on a blanket or two, and if this still isn't comfortable, then offer a block with a blanket over it to sit on. In some cases, students will complain about discomfort behind the knees which comes from a pulling at the hamstring attachments. Placing a blanket or rolled-up mat under the knees may bring the needed relief. At our studio we also offer large car wash sponges as a prop for a number of uses, including as a cushion under the knees in this pose.

In seated poses like Staff place a blanket under the pelvis for those with less flexible hamstrings and hips.

Another common complaint from students trying Staff is tension or even a burning sensation of the thighs near the hip joints. This is often the tensor fasciae latae (TFL) overworking. The TFL, along with other muscles, flexes, abducts, and medially rotates the hip. In an attempt to stabilize the hips in this posture a common pattern of movement sometimes occurs where the TFL overcompensates for other muscles, including the muscles of our core.

By taking a moment to support the torso with the hands on the mat, engage the core, and let the legs turn out in order to relax the TFL, we can start the process of undoing this pattern of movement where the TFL overworks.

Practice: Staff

1. Sit with your legs straight out in front of you. If you are uncomfortable, then stack two blankets up and sit on them. If you are uncomfortable behind the knees, then bend them and place a rolled-up blanket or large car wash sponges under them.
2. Place your fingertips on the mat to either side of your pelvis, and use your hands and shoulders to support yourself as you sit up as straight as you can.
3. Get your "yoga toes" going, pressing your big toe mounds forward a little as if you are pressing on the gas pedal and extending your other toes back toward you. Feel the energy coming into your arches and then up into your legs and hips.
4. Firm your thighs and keep them engaged.
5. Draw your low belly in and up, toning your abdominals.
6. Remember to breathe! Since your abdominals are working to help you stay erect, you can't do abdominal breathing. Instead, feel the breath moving the ribs.
7. If your hips and back are less flexible, then your legs may be rolling outward (laterally rotating like a dancer turning out) so that your toes are also pointing outward. If so, then tone your inner thighs towards the floor to help your knees and toes point as straight up as possible.
8. Resist the urge to round your back. Focus on sitting up and elongating your spine.
9. As you hold the pose and breathe, try pointing your feet and then deeply flexing your ankles, noticing any differences in how you experience the pose.
10. If your thighs begin to grip or burn near your hips, continue to support yourself with your hands, and then let your legs turn out for a few breaths to relax your hip flexors.
11. Engage your core by lifting the pit of your abdomen in and up while you slowly rotate your hips back to a neutral position

with your knees and toes pointing upward. By focusing on the core, you can reduce the burning sensation in the legs.

Focus + Daily Care

Focusing on the feet during yoga classes may help encourage students to take better care of their feet in general. How our feet function affects our gait and in turn how our legs, hips, and backs feel. The discomfort caused by even small warts and corns can affect our gait subtly and in turn create pain in our knees and hips. Yoga practice helps us to realize how important it is to quickly address foot issues. We also start to notice how awful our feet feel in poorly fitting shoes and high heels. Taking the time daily to walk around barefoot and care for our feet is time well spent. Love your feet and they will love you.

3

ALIGNING THE FEET AND ANKLES WITH THE KNEES

Alignment of the feet, ankles, and knees isn't important in just the standing postures. It is also important in all the poses, including those done seated. Our knees in particular are often an area of complaint for students before they even start yoga. For many people, daily patterns of movement, postural habits, and alignment negatively impact their joints. Excess weight alone can do damage as it puts so much pressure on knees and ankles. When excess weight is combined with unhealthy posture and alignment, the damage becomes unavoidable. Yoga can help us become more aware and begin to use better alignment throughout our daily activities. A good start is to focus on a particular part of the body in the postures and notice how it feels. When does it hurt? When does it feel good?

In this chapter we will discuss safe alignment of the knees and feet, how students distribute weight through their ankles and feet in the postures, and hyperextension of the knees. We will also discuss why in general the knees determine where the feet should be placed and not vice versa. Finding ways to guide students into an awareness of their feet and how they distribute their body weight in the standing postures can have huge, lifelong benefits.

ANKLE ALIGNMENT

The feet and the ankles obviously can't really be separated, so keep in mind our discussions from the last chapter about the feet as we move up to the ankles. Most of us have one of two patterns of walking: either we roll in on our ankles, putting more weight on the inside of our feet (pronation), or we roll out, putting more weight on the outside of our feet (supination). Many students have heard of these terms while shopping for shoes, but often don't really understand the concept or what to do about it. In pronation the arches and the inner ankle drop down, while supinated the arches and the inner ankles lift up. A silly way to remember this is to imagine the arches of the feet lifting up and wrapping around a bowl of soup (soup-ination). A person's feet don't necessarily have to match, as one foot can pronate while the other foot supinates.

Evidence of these patterns can be seen in the hips and shoulders. Keep this in mind as we move up the body focusing on individual parts, as each area is part of the whole system. What happens in the feet happens in the hips and the shoulders. Through yoga we can help ourselves and our students discover inefficient patterns of movement that we can address and hopefully improve.

Practice: Discovering Supination and Pronation

Set up your smartphone on the floor, leaning it against a wall or piece of furniture, and turn on the video recorder. If you don't have access to a smartphone, then set up a mirror so you can see your feet. Start to walk in place in front of the camera. Try not to think about how you are walking, just try to relax and move like you always do. If you are already deeply into yoga, then stop doing your yoga for a moment and see if you can capture how your feet move when you don't think about them. After walking in place for a few breaths, stop and just stand for a moment and notice where the weight is heaviest on your feet. If you start to adjust the weight right away, then walk in place again and try to catch yourself in that moment when you stop walking. Focus on one foot and then the other. Is the weight on the outside or inside of your foot? Is the inner ankle higher than the outer ankle? Watch the video and see what it might reveal. Enlist a friend to watch you if you are not sure, as they can look from different angles.

Working the Ankles and Feet with Awareness

Once students have an idea of their pattern of standing and walking, they can begin to correct it in the poses. In the standing poses if you tend to roll in on one or both feet (pronate), then focus on pressing into the outer heel to engage the muscles of the outer side of the foot, ankle, leg, and hip. If you tend to roll out on one or both feet (supinate), then focus on pressing into the big toe mound to engage the muscles of the inner side of the foot, ankle, and inner thigh. Where we press into the feet affects what muscles are engaging in the legs and hips. For instance, pressing into the outer heel helps to activate gluteus medius, which in turn can help lift the hip pointer and the arch. (We will talk more about the glutes and the hips in Chapter 5.) Weight evenly distributed throughout the feet creates a more balanced use of all our hip and leg muscles.

I tend to pronate a lot. Before I got into yoga, I learned that I pronated when I went to get running shoes and the knowledgeable clerk pointed it out. He put me in shoes with higher arch support so that when I walked my ankles would remain stable. At the time, I hardly paid attention to why he put me in those shoes. I know now I wasn't alone in this lack of awareness of my body. Many people are unaware of these alignment issues. Once I began to practice yoga, I soon realized that my habit of pronating was a factor not only when I walked or practiced standing yoga poses, but in almost everything I did. After a few years of consistent yoga and studying I discovered that my pronation was part of a bigger pattern that included an anterior pelvic tilt (the top of my pelvis tips forward and my low back arches). The awareness of my feet and ankles led me to begin to correct this postural habit, and to discover that my movement patterns had been causing me to experience low back pain. Some students might become aware of their hips first, and then it will lead to their feet; there are many ways into connection with the body.

TEACHING WARRIOR 1 WITH A FOCUS ON THE FEET AND KNEES

As you work through this book, many cues will be described that could be integrated into the steps below for Warrior 1. In other words, these steps are a start for working with deeper awareness in this pose. Some of the directions and cues I've used are not traditional. For many years, students have been taught to square the hips to the front of the mat in Warrior 1. The problem with this traditional approach is that squaring the hips to the front can put excessive pressure on the back knee, and for some students it causes discomfort in the area of the sacrum. In the practice below, I offer an option of leaving one hip back some, rather than squaring the pelvis to the front, and then rotating the ribs a little towards the front of the mat. This option helps prevent knee discomfort and other problems that traditional alignment in Warrior 1 may cause. Another option is to modify the pose to be a high lunge, lifting up the back heel entirely with the back leg in parallel (not turned out), and then squaring the hips to the front. In this option, the pose is more about working the thigh muscles and loses the great stretch that having the back heel down provides. For some students though, the high lunge option is really the best for them, especially if they've had knee surgeries, undiagnosed knee pain, or sacral pain.

It is common for teachers to ask students to "stack" the knee over the ankle of the bent knee in Warrior 1, Warrior 2, and Side Angle. In the past this alignment was considered safer, but more teachers have come to the conclusion that stacking the knee over the ankle is more about aesthetics, as it creates nice lines. When we walk, run, climb stairs, or squat, our knees go out past our ankles and even past our toes sometimes. It is a natural movement. In the standing poses, what is most important is that the students are grounded in their heels and big toe mounds, and that the joints of their knees and hips are comfortable. If the feet are grounded, then the knee will only go so far past the toes, so there isn't a safety issue in this case. I cue students to bend their knees, so they feel challenged in their thighs, but there is no pinching or pain in their joints.

Another alignment debate continues between teachers about whether the back foot in Warrior 1 should be cued to 45 degrees or some other angle. When we cue specific angles for the back foot in this pose, it puts the focus on the aesthetics of the pose rather than how students feel in it. Due to structural differences, not all students can safely plant their back foot in the same position in Warrior 1. When a student plants their back foot first at 45 degrees and then tries to square their hips to the front of the mat, the back knee is often torqued. This same issue arises with poses that face the long side of the mat such as Triangle and Side Angle. When students attempt to square the hips to the side of the mat after planting their feet, they will often feel this in one or both of their knees. The knees are at the mercy of what happens in the relationship between the feet/ankles and the hips. During transitions between poses, students' knees are less at risk if we ask them to pivot on the heels or big toe mounds as they turn the hips in or out. Over the years I've learned to cue from the hips[1] first and let the knees and toes follow.

Practice: Warrior 1

1. Starting in Mountain with your hands on your hips, take a comfortable step back with your right foot, then place your heels in a line or a little wider.
2. Turn your right hip out to a comfortable amount by pivoting on your right big toe mound, and then let your knees and toes follow that turn-out. Readjust the alignment of your heels if needed.
3. Ground through both sides of the feet, feeling the big toe mounds and the outer heels connecting with the floor.

Imagine rooting the feet into the mat and lifting energy into the arches.

4. Bend the front knee to a comfortable position, somewhere over the ankle. Your right hip will be a little farther back than your left hip. Leave it where your hips and sacrum are comfortable, not forcing it forward.
5. Stay grounded in your back outer heel and big toe mound and keep engaging your back quadriceps and gluteal muscles.
6. Leave your right hip where it is, tone your low belly a little to the right, then add a little twist in the ribs towards the left so that your rib cage is facing the front of your mat.
7. Lift your arms up over your head with your hands around shoulder-width apart or wider and with the palms facing each other. If the shoulders are uncomfortable, bring them a little forward of the body.
8. Keep the arms active, imagining that you are hugging a ball between them.
9. Keep breathing gently into the ribs, making your exhales last at least as long as your inhales.
10. Keep your back heel connected to the floor. For those that pronate, this is especially important to counter the tendency of the inner ankles to drop down and the outer heel to come up.
11. Notice that you can be physically working to stay in the pose, and yet also be relaxed watching the breath come in and out. Be aware of what sensations you feel.
12. Connect with the lines of energy coming from the feet into the legs and hips. Imagine lines of energy from both the inner and outer ankles running up your legs into your pelvis.
13. To come out of the pose, keep your core engaged while placing your hands on your hips and taking a step forward with your right foot to return to Mountain.

ANKLE RANGE OF MOTION ONLY PART OF THE STORY WITH SQUAT

Although squatting down to pick something up or weed the garden is a natural human movement, for many people it's very hard to do without discomfort in the hips, knees, or ankles. Everyone can benefit from improving their ability to squat, hopefully making yard chores and other daily activities more comfortable. In yoga class, however, the litany of complaints begins whenever we start teaching Squat. Often students' heels pop up off the floor, and the fronts of their ankles start to hurt as they struggle to stay in the posture. Due to this, the range of motion (ROM) of the ankles is often blamed for this inability to squat. If the student has healthy knees and hips that have a full ROM, then indeed it may be their ankles keeping them from getting into a deep Squat. As their teacher, we can guide them to discover whether this ROM issue is related to their bony structure or muscular restriction. The ankles have to be able to flex enough for the knees to come out over the toes in this posture. One in six students will likely not have the ability to flex their ankles enough — due to their bone structure — to ever be able to squat without a blanket or wedge under their heels.[2]

For other students the restriction is due to less flexible calves, and students will make progress by simply practicing standing postures like Pyramid and Standing Forward Bend. For students with less flexible calves than average, we can guide them through specific calf stretches that may help. We will cover those later in this chapter. The ankles though are only part of the story when it comes to Squat.

How long it takes a student to comfortably be in a squat will vary greatly depending not only on the ROM of their ankles but also of their hips and knees. In order to squat well, the hips must be able to flex deeply, with the knees close to the chest or each side of the chest depending on the variation of the pose. For students who are frustrated with their hips in Squat, remind them that all the standing poses help to warm and open the hips. They can continue to work with classic hip opening poses like Pigeon, Lizard, and Cobbler as they make gradual progress over time. The knees must also fully flex in order for students to be able to hold a deep Squat. If the student has any previous knee issues or surgeries, then it may not be worth the risk of working on the deep version of this pose.

Offer a more accessible version of Squat by placing a rolled up blanket under the heels. Holding a block or another prop out in front helps to counterbalance the pelvis.

No matter whether it is the hips, knees, ankles, or some combination of the three, most students who struggle with Squat will benefit from placing a rolled-up blanket under their heels. Some studios have wedges which are also helpful in this situation, but if your place of work lacks these props, then a rolled-up yoga mat also works great. Even with good ROM in all of these joints, some students may struggle due to their body proportions. If a student has a heavy pelvis and a shorter, lighter torso, then they may not be able to get enough counterbalance between the upper body and lower body to squat without support under the heels. In addition, a tight lower back can affect the ability to move the upper body forward enough to counterbalance a larger, heavier pelvis. For these students, a block or heavier exercise ball held out in front of them will help to counterbalance the pelvis.

In the struggle to get into Squat students may try various compensations, like turning their hips way out, or letting their knees splay out too far to the side. It is fine to let students try changing the width of their stance, or turning their hips out some, but we need to avoid extreme compensations and encourage them to keep the big toe mounds and outer heels grounded into the mat or the prop to avoid supination and pronation.

Let's look at some cueing to guide students towards improving their Squat and maybe even liking it a little better over time.

Practice: Modified Squat

1. Roll up a yoga blanket or a mat. Place the rolled-up prop under your heels and stand with your feet a little wider than hip width apart.
2. Turn your hips out slightly, letting your knees and toes follow the turn-out.
3. Hold a block or an exercise ball out in front of you at about heart height.
4. Support yourself with your core by drawing the pit of the abdomen in and up.
5. Start to bend your knees, letting your knees track over your toes, and drop your pelvis down as far as you can go.
6. Keep holding the prop out in front of you to help counterbalance yourself until you can learn to squat without it.
7. Notice how your knees and hips feel; if something hurts, then

try coming back up and adjust the width of your stance or the turn-out of your hips a little.

8. Continue to ground your heels onto the rolled-up prop while grounding your big toe mounds into the mat and keeping even weight on both sides of your feet.
9. Let the area around the sacrum get heavy and drop down toward the floor.
10. If you are less flexible in your lower back, then this could be keeping you from moving your upper body forward enough to counterbalance with the pelvis. Try imagining that you are breathing into your low back for a possible release.
11. Once settled into the pose, lengthen your spine as best as you can and breathe into your ribs.
12. To come out of the pose, place the prop in your hands on the floor, and bring your hands to your hips. Take a big inhale, and as you exhale press strongly into your heels to stand up. Another option for coming out of a Squat is to place blocks in front of you and put your hands on them. Then lift your pelvis up to come into a Standing Forward Bend while keeping your knees slightly bent. Place your hands on your hips and return to Mountain.

Opening the Calves for a Deeper Squat

When I first started yoga, I would often avoid Squat and other poses where I had to stretch my calves, without an awareness of why I didn't like those poses. As my practice developed, I learned that my lower calves were particularly tight, and basic yoga poses alone were not resulting in the release I wanted. Although the calves are stretched in standing postures such as Warrior 1 and 2, Side Angle, and Triangle, certain areas of the calves can be easily ignored or circumvented if the heel rises up a little or the position of the hips is changed to avoid the tight area.

It is worthwhile to add some basic calf stretches to our classes to address common calf tightness. I like to start students with the basic "runners stretch" at the wall. Have students place their hands on the wall and take a comfortable step back with one foot. Remind them to press equally into the big toe mounds and the outer heels to avoid supination and pronation. In this basic variation, it is most common to keep the back leg straight as we lean towards the wall stretching the big calf muscle (gastrocnemius). Another variation is to have students shorten their stance a bit, and then keeping their heels grounded, bend both knees a little. This takes the stretch into the lower part of the calf (soleus).

For those who can tolerate holding forward bends, I share the calf stretches below from my own practice which includes standing on a rolled-up blanket and then dropping my heels to the mat as I forward fold. After finishing up your calf stretches, try your Squat again to see if it makes the pose more comfortable. Some students will feel no difference. Others will experience a noticeable improvement.

Practice: Calf Stretches to Help with Squat

1. Take a yoga blanket or a yoga mat and roll it up like you did for your Squat. Place your feet on the roll so the arches are right on top of the roll and so your toes and heels drape over the front and back of the roll.
2. Now slowly lower your heels onto the floor. The toe mounds and some of your arches will still be on the roll.
3. Bend your knees and see if you can get your hands onto some blocks, a chair seat, or the floor. If it feels like too much, then undo your roll some to lower the toe mounds.
4. Try straightening your legs, keeping your hands on the blocks or a chair if needed. Notice how the stretch changes if your knees are straight or bent.
5. As you ground your heels into the floor imagine that you are lifting your inner and outer ankles up, making some space at the front of the ankle.
6. Activate your thighs gently to keep them toned, and remember to breathe.

7. If you find that you are fairly comfortable in this position, then try standing up and turning your hips out some and let your knees and toes follow the turn-out. Keep your big toe mounds on the roll and your heels on the floor.
8. Forward fold again and put your hands on the blocks or floor. Notice if you feel the stretch change, and again try it with both straight and bent knees.
9. Come to standing again, and try turning your hips internally just a little, letting the knees and toes follow as if you were pigeon toed. Keep your big toe mounds on the roll and your heels on the floor.
10. Being mindful of your knees, forward bend again and ground your fingertips onto the floor. Pay attention to how the stretch changes. Try both straight and bent knees in this position.
11. Try your squat again now and see if these stretches made any difference for you.

AVOIDING MENISCUS TEARS

Clearly, students are not generally experiencing dramatic knee injuries like ACL tears in the middle of yoga classes. These serious ligament injuries are more common in contact sports where the knee gets hit from the front or side. However, by encouraging healthy knee alignment, we are more likely to prevent one of the most generally common injuries, the torn meniscus.

The menisci are crescent-shaped rubbery discs that stabilize our knee joints. Athletes experience a torn meniscus when the knee is twisted in contact sports. In yoga, the tears can occur whenever the knee is caught in a battle between the thigh (femur) and the lower leg (tibia) going in different directions. This can happen in yoga when students pivot the feet around during an active flow class, especially if the flow is fast paced and the student is struggling to keep up. One way of cueing in this situation is to educate students to pivot on their heels and then cue from the hips. After coming up from Wide-Legged Forward Fold to a standing wide position an example cue to transition to Warrior 2 could include, "Pivot on your left heel while turning your left hip out." Once the students learn to pivot on the heels, a cue could include, "turn your left hip out, letting the knees and toes follow." In some transitions, students might find it easier to pivot on their big toe mounds rather than their heels. This also works as long as the movement starts from the hip and the knees and toes turn together.

As we age, the menisci slowly deteriorate in many individuals, which makes a tear much more likely. With older, more brittle menisci, even twisting the knee getting out of the car can cause a tear. For older students and new students, slowing the pace down for standing poses and flows is the best practice. This allows extra time to transition between the poses, where a twisted knee is most likely to occur. During balancing poses, use the wall or chairs for support to avoid twisting the knees as the students struggle to stand on one foot.

The knee can also be twisted in poses like Warrior 2, Triangle, and Side Angle when the front foot is planted, and then the student attempts to square the hips to the side of the mat. Most students do not have the ability to open their hips far enough to square the pelvis to the side of the mat, so with the foot planted the pressure goes to the common weak link, the knee joint.[3] It is best to cue the knee to track with the toes first in this situation, and then let the student leave their hips where they are comfortable. See the detailed cueing ideas for Triangle in Chapter 4 and Side Angle in Chapter 8 for avoiding squaring the hips to the side of the mat.

Two other poses where students are at risk for injury due to twisting the knee are Pigeon (example in Chapter 5) and Lotus. In Pigeon, the knee can be twisted when students try to place the front shin parallel to the front of the mat and then bring their pelvis down, putting pressure on the knee. A similar twisting of the knee happens in Lotus when students pull a foot up and over the opposite leg. They are pulling the tibia up while forcing the femur into a rotation, and if they do not have enough ability to laterally rotate the hip, the pressure will again go to the knee.

HYPEREXTENSION OF THE KNEE

Hyperextension or hypermobility of the joints is an inherited condition that affects many joints in the body, not just the knee. Students who are hypermobile may have more joint pain or be more easily injured. Strengthening the muscles around the hypermobile joint can reduce injuries and inflammation. Hyperextension of the knee is when the knee "locks out" and the joint starts to move backwards. In extreme cases, when looking from the side, the knee can look like it is going the wrong way or is "double-jointed." In many cases, the quadriceps are not as active when the knee "locks out" into hyperextension, and this puts additional pressure on the joint, especially in standing postures. Toning and building up the muscles of the legs can reduce the amount of hyperextension in some cases.

Whenever a person who hyperextends their knees hears "straighten your legs," they often hyperextend even more, as in their mind that is what straight feels like. Their proprioception of their own knee joint is not quite calibrated correctly. Proprioception is the ability to perceive and feel where your body parts and joints are in relationship to each other. Your proprioceptors tell your brain where your body is in space. Students who hyperextend their knees have to start thinking of softening their knees or even creating a micro-bend whenever they hear "straighten your legs." Although in their minds it will feel like their legs are bent, observers will tell them their legs are straight. Over time, hypermobile students learn to back off and protect their joints. If a student walks in and immediately places their palms on the floor in Standing Forward Fold along with hyperextended knees, then our job as their teacher is to try to convince them of another way to practice. They don't need to get any more flexible to be healthy, they need to build strength and stability. Let's explore cues for the hypermobile in Standing Forward Fold.

Practice: Standing Forward Fold for the Hypermobile Student

1. Stand at the front of your mat in Mountain. Press your feet evenly into your mat and gently firm your quadriceps and glutes.
2. Elongate your back, reaching long through the crown of your head.
3. Bring your hands to your hips and bend your knees a little. Imagine you are moving your legs and feet away from each other, as if you are trying to stretch the mat a little wider.
4. Keep that firmness and action gently going as you fold forward at the hips keeping your spine long. As you fold forward, work to keep your hips over your feet rather than letting them shift backwards.
5. Although you may easily reach the floor with your hands, place your hands on blocks and focus on engaging your muscles.
6. Continue keeping your knees a little bent and let yourself fold forward further, possibly bringing your fingertips to the floor.
7. Feel energy coming into your arches and rising up into your legs and hips.
8. Tone your low belly, drawing it in a little and lifting it up.
9. Lengthen your upper back and avoid rounding over at first, working for an active pose rather than collapsing into it.
10. If you want to go as deep as bringing your palms to the floor, then continue to firm your legs while keeping a little bend in the knees.
11. As you fold deeper, imagine your sit bones are connecting with your heels, activating your hamstrings. For those who are very deep in the forward bend, this may also create a feeling of a little space at the front of the hips.
12. To come out of the pose, keep your knees bent and imagine

you are making your mat a little wider by working your feet and legs away from each other. Keep that action going, then place your hands on your hips and with a straight back come up to standing.

THE KNEES AND TOES IN ONE-LEGGED BALANCES

When students struggle with balancing, it's often helpful to focus on the feet for a moment. The cue to "point the toes straight forward" doesn't always work for everyone. Some of us are built such that our feet turn out very slightly when we walk. The way to check on this in class is to have everyone stand with their feet under the hips and with their toes pointing straight forward. Then bend the knees and see where they track. For some students the knees will then bend towards each other rather than tracking with the toes. When the knees track inward like this, the whole pose is less stable, and it puts unnecessary pressure on the joints. I'm suggesting just a little bit of a turn-out of the toes, not a full lateral rotation of the hip like first position in dance. With this little turn-out of the feet, have them bend the knees again, and for some people the knees will now track with their toes and balancing will be immensely easier. Explore this option in poses like Tree, Dancer, Big Toe Hold, and Warrior 3.

LINING UP THE KNEES IN GODDESS

Traditionally the Goddess was taught with a huge turnout of the hips. The pose is really just an upright squat, which is great for building strength as long as we cue it safely. When students try to follow their flexible teachers into Goddess, their knees often drift inward. This is because they turn their toes way out and plant their feet first, and then their hips do not have the ROM to line up with the feet. As we discussed earlier in this chapter, when the feet and the hips are going in different directions, the knees can suffer. Sometimes students also torque their ankles to make their toes point outward more in an attempt to mirror the hypermobile aesthetic. Since this pose has traditionally been about the lateral rotation of the hips, it is even more important to cue from the hips first, pivoting on the heels. In an attempt to turn out and keep the knees and toes in line, some students will arch their low back and stick their buttocks out behind them (fondly known as "perky butt" at our studio). In this instance, they just need to come up, reduce the turn-out, and then drop back into the pose.

Practice: Goddess

1. Take a comfortable, wide stance while facing the long side of your mat.
2. With your hands on your hips, pivot on one heel and then the other while turning the hips out and letting the knees and feet follow that turn-out.
3. Ground the outer heels and the big toe mounds, rooting the feet and feeling the arches lift.
4. Keeping the torso upright, bend the knees while letting them track with the middle of the feet. Avoid going past the toes with your knees keeping your heels grounded.
5. Draw the pit of the abdomen in and up while also keeping your upper abdominals firm and avoiding your lower ribs shifting forward.
6. Focus on a nice, long spine. If you feel your low back going into a backbend or you know you are lordotic (swaybacked), then imagine your sacrum getting heavy, releasing your back muscles some and firming your glutes. If you still feel like you are arching your back, then come out of the pose, reduce your turn-out and try again.
7. Lift the arms up into a T position and bend the elbows into cactus position, facing the palms forward.
8. Take your elbows up slightly higher than your shoulders. Feel the muscles on your upper back around the shoulder blades working, rather than gripping in your neck.
9. If you feel tension in your knees, or feel the knees drifting

toward the midline past your big toes, then come out of the pose and make the turn-out of your hips less and then drop back into the pose again.

10. To come out of the pose, press into your heels and keep your core active as you straighten your legs and bring your arms to your side.

Slow Down + Offer Options

The ROM of our students' joints are different, and so to teach the safest mixed level classes we need to offer options. Cues that try to force all bodies into the same position, including "squaring the pelvis to the side of the mat," and specific angles for the feet, can cause injury to the knees. Slowing down the pace of our classes so that new students have time to process what they are hearing makes the experience more accessible and reduces injuries.

4

ACTIVATING THE QUADRICEPS AND GLUTES

Learning to activate the quadriceps (thighs) and glutes (buttocks) in the poses was the hardest movement fundamental for me to learn in the beginning. Even today I often must remind myself to firm up my glutes in certain poses. Activating these muscles in seated poses is a particular challenge when teaching new students who are used to just relaxing and stretching at the end of a fitness class. In this chapter, we will give examples of this fundamental in various poses, offer creative imagery for guiding students to connect with their muscles, and share teaching ideas. We will also discuss working with students who overuse their glutes.

Some commonly used basic language for many of the poses is "firm" or "engage" the thighs and glutes. I've also heard the cues "tighten," "squeeze," or "activate" the muscles. Although this seems like a simple task, students struggle with grasping this concept in a static pose, and once they do understand they often have trouble remembering or finding the motivation. It's easier to just hang out in Triangle on our bones and not use our muscles much at all. In addition, the intensity of the firming or engaging can really vary, with some students overdoing it while others are not really working. We want to help them find some middle ground in their activation, firming without gripping or creating too much tension.

Since students struggle to learn and remember this foundational element, teachers have created various cues and imagery for it over the years. One of the first cues I remember hearing from some older teachers was, “lift your kneecaps up.” At first, I thought they were pretty crazy. It was only later that I realized if I focused on using my thigh muscles to try and lift my kneecaps up my quadriceps would firm up. Another popular cue I heard in some of the standing poses like Warrior 2 and Side Angle was, “imagine you are lifting your foot off the mat, but you can’t.” That one works even if you are seated in a chair — imagine you are trying to lift your feet off the floor and feel how your quadriceps engage.

Let’s look first at Triangle and work in some basic cues to help guide students into an awareness of what they are doing in the pose. Some students forget about their back leg and let it go soft while shifting more of their weight on the front leg. Others keep equal weight on both feet but don't actively use their muscles, relying instead on just stacking their bones and balancing that way. Unengaged quadriceps are also often seen when students hyperextend their knees. The challenge is to find cueing that encourages them to engage while also stretching and feeling the lines of energy in all directions.

Practice: Triangle

1. Stand in Mountain while facing the long side of your mat. Place your hands on your hips and take a wide stance that is comfortable.
2. Turn your left hip out, pivoting on your heel, and let your knees and toes follow so that your toes point towards the front of the mat.
3. Turn your right hip inward a little, pivoting on your big toe mound, and let the knees and toes follow so that the back right heel is a little further back than the big toe mound. If this

is uncomfortable for your right knee, then let your right hip be neutral with the knees and toes pointing towards the long side of your mat.

4. Place your heels in a line or a little wider.
5. Shift your weight from foot to foot a few times, feeling the ground, and find a place where you feel equal weight on both feet.
6. Spread the toes out and ground through the big toe mounds and the outer heels. Imagine you are drawing energy coming up through the arches into the hips and pelvis.
7. Imagine you are lifting your kneecaps up as you firm the muscles of your thighs and your calves. Remember to firm the thighs on both the front and back leg.
8. Connect to your outer heels and actively press them into the mat and gently away from each other while keeping the big toe mounds firmly grounded. Imagine you are trying to make your mat longer by working the thighs away from each other.
9. See if you can create an energetic connection between your sit bones and your heels to help firm the glutes and the backs of your legs. Imagine that you are reaching your sit bones towards your heels without actually letting the bones move.
10. Draw your front hip pointers (ASIS) together while you bring the pit of the abdomen in and up and then lengthen through the crown of your head, elongating your spine.
11. Take an inhale into your ribs to prepare, and then exhale as you fold lower over your left leg, keeping a long spine. When you fold as far as you can comfortably, let your torso stop there and elongate your spine. Bring your left hand to a block or the floor just to the outside of your left ankle. As you fold over, avoid leaning your torso forward or shifting your pelvis behind you.
12. Come onto the fingertips of the left hand and keep a feeling of energy lifting up from the palms as you take a little bit of weight into your left hand and shoulder.
13. At first, leave your right hand on your right hip and work on

keeping your rib cage hovering directly over your left leg. Continue elongating your spine. Then start to rotate your rib cage upward, moving the sternum a little bit toward the ceiling. As you begin rotating your rib cage upward, keep your hips still.

14. Reach your right arm up with your palm facing forward and keep your hand above or slightly in front of your shoulder.
15. Imagine the energy moving into your legs and arms, reaching your limbs long in all directions.
16. To come out of the pose, keep your muscles firm and take an inhale to prepare. Bring your hands to your hips and on the exhale soften your knees a little and imagine you are working your legs and feet away from each other as you bring your torso up.

Looking down at the floor in Triangle is an option that may be easier on some students' necks.

TEACHING NOTES ON TRIANGLE

With the front hip laterally rotating and the back hip medially rotating, this basic pose is great for warming up the hips and legs before doing more difficult hip-opening poses such as Pigeon. When teaching students Triangle, the first challenge is to help them understand that we want their torso directly over their front leg. In an attempt to get their bottom hand to the floor, students will often pitch themselves forward to get to the ground, both leaning forward and rounding their backs. Placing a block to the outside of the students' front ankle and having them put their fingertips on the block can help. Since students are often resistant to using props at first, it is best if the teacher uses a block to show the pose. Many years ago, a popular instruction for dealing with this pitching forward was to cue students to imagine they were standing between two panes of glass, but this cue has fallen out of favor as it doesn't take into account the average hip structure. Some students also have an emotional reaction, feeling tense or trapped between the glass. The idea behind the glass planes cue was not only to have the rib cage over the front leg, but also to "stack" the hips, with one hip directly over the other.

Cueing the stacking of the hips between the planes of glass still persists in some yoga circles, as it has been such a popular cue over the years. However, most people's hips cannot safely stack in this position. The majority of students will do better in Triangle with the top hip slightly forward of the bottom hip. Teachers that insist on coming up behind students and trying to pull the top hip directly over the bottom hip risk irritating and perhaps even injuring the student's hips and SI joints. It's better to let the top hip pointer (ASIS) move slightly downward and focus on engaging the abdominals.

If most of us cannot "stack" the hips in Triangle, then our rib cage will follow the hips and be facing slightly downward. This is just fine for those who are less flexible, as they can be in the pose comfortably. For those who can tolerate a twist in this pose we can rotate the rib cage upward with our sternum facing the walls or twist even further rotating our sternum towards the ceiling (see step #13 for Triangle above as an example). All of the asymmetrical standing poses will have little twists in them, unless we are more comfortable leaving the twist out and practicing the pose in a way that doesn't match the popular aesthetic.

Once we get the students into their version of Triangle, the next challenge is to encourage them to continue to firm their muscles. In addition to using clear verbal cues like "firm" or "engage" we can also try the classic cue "lift your kneecaps up" that was mentioned above. Instead of asking students to place their hand on the block or the floor, another option is to ask them to put their hand on their thigh, and then press their hand onto their thigh and their thigh back into their hand. This isometric cue of pressing into the thighs sometimes helps to get the point across. This same isometric cue can be done with the shin, by placing the lower hand in Triangle on the shin and pressing the shin back into the hand. In some trainings, teachers are encouraged not to let students put their hands on their shins in Triangle, as sometimes people dump their upper body weight on their shin putting too much pressure on the knee. For those that hyperextend, dumping the weight on the shin can be even harder on the knee. If we can get students to press the shin back up into the hand, and not lock the knee out, this cue is effective and safe to get the calves, thighs, and even the hamstrings working.

As we discussed in Chapter 3, the angle of the back foot isn't as important as how the knees and hips feel in the pose. Some students enjoy a slight medial rotation of the back hip in Triangle, others prefer the hip to be in neutral. As long as they can gently abduct the hips while engaging the thighs and glutes, and their joints are comfortable, exact angles and positions are not needed. Everyone's body cannot fit into the same form.

CREATIVE IMAGERY FOR ENGAGING THE LEGS

After new students come to class for a few months they will often stop listening to many of the cues they hear the teacher say. They think they already know what the teacher is talking about, or they never got it and just decided to ignore that particular cue. Sometimes they may believe they understand the instruction, but in reality don't have a clue what the teacher is talking about. Telling students to firm up their thighs in the poses and actually have them do it consistently takes a lot of repetition and change of language. In many cases students may not be ready yet to fully understand what the teacher wants. Becoming aware of the body and being able to access the ability to recruit certain muscles in specific positions takes time and practice. A person can intellectually understand that you want them to firm their thighs in a pose, and physically not be able to make it happen.

One classic cue that has been around for many years to encourage students to firm up their legs is "shin bone forward." When I first heard the cue, I had absolutely no idea what they were talking about. Only later as I began to understand the imagery did I realize they wanted me to imagine that I was moving my shin bone forward in space, but not really move it. Using the word "imagine" in a cue that includes imagery can help new students understand what is going on, rather than just saying shin bone forward. Another possibility is to have students place their hand on their shin and then ask them to press their shin into their hand as was mentioned above. This way they can experience what happens when they imagine their shin moving forward and feel the muscles in their legs activate. Once students understand what shin bone forward means, it's a great cue and reminder for them to keep working in the poses. In hindsight it makes me laugh at myself remembering when I first visited a class many years ago and heard a teacher say, "shin bone forward" and I literally moved my shin forward in space. I had no idea what he was talking about.

When some of my students didn't seem to be getting anywhere with the "shin bone forward" cue I thought about ways to say the same thing but talk about the muscles instead. One day while they were in Wide-Legged Forward Bend I said something like, "imagine the muscles of your calves are wrapping around to the back of your leg. Now feel the back of your calf firm and move forward. Feel the energy circling around from the front of the shin to the side of the calf and then back to the front of the shin. Like two cylinders are moving in your legs trying to push your shins forward." A number of people in the class reacted letting me know they felt something, and some students came up afterwards to tell me they felt the cylinders. Others were quite mystified as to what I was talking about, and so it goes with imagery. Those that realized I was just saying shin bones forward in a different way had moved into another level of understanding with the work.

MOBILIZING THE GLUTES

Many people go through their daily activities without actively using their buttock muscles, otherwise known as the glutes. When the glutes are not recruited to work at the right times, the body compensates and uses other muscles. Over time, this can cause pain, injury, and reduced athletic performance. In yoga, we can use specific cues to help get the glutes involved more actively in the poses. For example, in the standing poses we can cue grounding into the outer heels while pressing the legs and feet gently away from each other. A few years back a number of nationally known teachers, including my own, started teaching and publishing articles encouraging students to work their legs away from each other (abduction) in the standing poses, rather than the tradition of hugging them inward (adduction). Introducing abduction to beginners in the standing poses encourages them to use the buttocks muscles and stabilize the hips. When this is combined with grounding the heels and other imagery to tone all of the gluteal muscles, students gain strength and make progress more quickly.

A great example of how important it is to teach students to work their glutes is the challenging Warrior 3 pose. When trying Warrior 3 in the first few months of class, many students will let the knee on the standing leg track inward towards their big toe or the middle of their mat, while at the same time the hip on their standing leg drifts out to the side. Sometimes they will also turn their feet on the standing leg slightly inward. This misalignment is hard on the knees and also relies too much on the thighs, often leaving the biggest buttocks muscle, gluteus maximus, relaxed on the sidelines. The back leg that is extended behind in Warrior 3 can also be stabilized by engaging the buttocks muscles. If the glutes are not helping lift the back leg, then the hamstrings have to do more of the work, the low back is often strained, and it's harder to keep the pelvis stable.

Practice: Warrior 3

1. Place two blocks in front of your mat on their highest level.
2. Starting in Mountain at the front of your mat spread out your toes and feel your arches lift up. Stay balanced between your big toe mounds and your outer heels. Draw energy from your feet up into your legs and into your pelvis.
3. Begin to bring your weight onto your left foot, and let your right foot come just behind you on your mat like a kickstand on a bike.
4. Before folding forward into the pose, bend your left knee and let it track with your toes.
5. Press into your outer left heel and feel the upper buttocks engage as they stabilize your hip. While you are doing this, remember to also ground into your big toe mound.
6. Feel the pit of your abdomen lift in and up, toning your low belly.
7. Keeping your back long, fold forward at your hips, and place your fingers onto the blocks in front of you. Move the blocks so they are directly under your shoulders.
8. Keep your gaze on the floor and your head and neck in line

with your long spine. Avoid rounding your back, and bend one or both of your knees if you need to for comfort.

9. Lift your back leg long behind you with your back heel as high as your pelvis, or lower if needed. Slightly turn out your right hip, letting the knees and toes follow, to help tone your glutes.
10. Work on keeping your pelvis level with the ground even though your right hip is turned out. Imagine you have a teacup resting on the back of your pelvis and you don't want it to spill.
11. Spread your right toes creating "yoga toes." Draw energy into your right leg, starting with your arch and firming your right thigh.
12. On your left leg, feel the sit bone getting heavy as it energetically connects downward toward your heel.
13. On your right leg, try to recreate that same feeling you found in your standing (left) leg imagining the sit bone reaching towards the heel.
14. Feel your upper abdominals just below your ribs firming as you scoop your lowest ribs inward and upwards, while keeping a long neutral spine.
15. Elongate your spine, reaching the crown of your head one way while you reach your pelvis in the other direction. Imagine your rib cage is moving away from your pelvis as your spine lengthens, making your waist longer.
16. Work to slowly straighten your legs as much as you can without anything hurting.
17. Once you feel engaged and stable, lift your hands to your heart or even stretch them out over your head.
18. To come out of the pose, take an inhale to prepare, and then on your exhale keep your muscles activated as you bring your right foot to the floor under your right hip. Bend your knees and bring your hands to your hips. While gently engaging the legs and feet away from each other and maintaining a long spine, come up to standing.

TEACHING NOTES ON WARRIOR 3

Starting students with blocks in this pose works well to help them find safe alignment before trying to hold the position. Warrior 3 is one of the hardest standing poses, and students will go to familiar patterns of moving to try and stretch their arms over their head.

Build strength while working towards Warrior 3 with one hand grounded on a block and the other extended creating an opposite arm leg balance.

Only the most athletic people will be able to do the full version of this pose correctly on the first day, and even they may struggle with alignment.

Traditionally, Warrior 3 has been taught with the standing foot pointing exactly straight forward, but as we discussed in Chapter 3 this doesn't work for everyone. Although we do want that foot pointing mostly forward, we need to allow a little room for adjustment, depending on the different shapes of people's feet and the way in which they naturally walk. Some people walk with their feet pointing ever so slightly out, and their knees track right with their feet. These students will balance better if we let their feet turn out a little, as this is how they are naturally built. Other students may try to come into Warrior 3 pointing the toes on their standing leg inward. Sometimes this is caused by the TFL (tensor fascia latae) overworking in an attempt to stabilize the hip. In this case, we can cue the student to turn their hip out a little, letting the knees and toes follow, and ask them to recruit their gluteus maximus. Getting the largest glutes working in Warrior 3 often takes the pinch out of the hip that many students complain about. In summary, we want the hips and feet working together to keep the knees tracking with the feet. If the standing foot is forced to go in a different direction than the hip in this pose, then the knee is put under stress.

Another one of the most common misalignments in Warrior 3 happens when one hip is held higher than the other hip. If the student is standing on their left foot with the right leg lifted behind them, it's often the right hip that rises up higher. When this happens, they are using the muscles of the outer hip on the standing left leg to stabilize the pose, and they are not working as hard in the abdominals or glutes on the right side. The same solution as mentioned above often works in this situation also. Let the right hip turn out ever so slightly and focus on recruiting the gluteus maximus in the pose. Although it is not the traditional aesthetic in this posture (knees and toes pointing straight downward on the lifted leg), it's more effective in helping beginners learn to engage their glutes and level the pelvis.

When the teacher asks them to engage the glutes and lower the right hip, this is followed by some gasping and complaining when the students realize how hard it is to practice the pose this way. The more the right hip is lifted, the closer Warrior 3 starts to resemble Half Moon. Students will truly believe their hips are level even when they are not. Sometimes the best way to break through to someone is to ask them to stay for a moment after class or meet them for a private session and take a picture of them in the pose. When they see the picture, a strong reaction may follow: "I had no idea I was doing that!"

CREATIVE IMAGERY FOR ENGAGING THE GLUTES WITHOUT THE GRIPPING

If a student hasn't been using their buttock muscles enough, then when they start to engage more, they may at first grip the buttocks together. Over gripping of the cheeks usually causes the pelvis to go into a posterior pelvic tilt, which is not the best position for many asanas. There is a difference between engaging the glutes with a feeling of energy flowing downward toward the ground and engaging them so tightly that both sides of the buttocks feel like they are moving toward the midline and clenching together.

At the other end of the spectrum, there are some individuals who grip the buttock muscles too much in their daily activities. Although not as common, this pattern of movement sometimes contributes to the development of low back and SI joint problems. With these students, the cues for learning to engage the glutes may not be helpful. They instead need to learn to relax the buttocks first, and then practice toning without the gripping. Overusing the glutes often flattens the low back, and these students need to learn to release and bring a natural curve back to their lumbar spine.

We can use similar language in class with both of these types of students, to try and impart the idea of toning the glutes without over-doing it. Of course, trying to talk about the buttocks can be awkward and often brings giggles in class. When this happens, I try to go with the flow and crack a few jokes I've heard other teachers say, such as "try not to crack a walnut back there," or "if you are holding the winning lottery ticket back there, then let it go," or an oldie but goodie, "tone like a grape, not like a watermelon!"

How do we teach students to flow the glutes downward rather than gripping them in? A repetition of reminders not to grip may work for a while, but students will often stop listening if the same cue is always used. Bringing them to the front of their mat for a short teaching moment in Mountain pose often helps.

Practice: Feeling the Glutes Working Downward Rather than Gripping Together

1. Stand in Mountain with your hands on your hips and your pelvis in a neutral position. Connect with your breathing, creating relaxed inhales and exhales.
2. Soften your knees a little and ground through your big toe mounds and your outer heels.
3. With your hands on your hips, place your thumbs a little lower so you can feel the top of your glutes.
4. Press actively into your outer heels to firm up the upper part of your buttock (gluteus medius).
5. Keeping your pelvis in a neutral position, imagine your sacrum is getting heavy.
6. If you feel your pelvis moving and your low back flattening, then place one hand on your low belly and the back of the other hand on your lumbar curve. Gently hold your pelvis in neutral as you try the imagery in step #5 and step #7.
7. Imagine your sit bones are reaching towards your heels, as energy flows from the back of your pelvis all the way to the floor. Avoid "tucking the tailbone" or feeling your pelvis move into a posterior tilt.
8. Continue pressing into your big toe mounds and outer heels and then also try imagining that the bottom of your pelvis around the sit bones is filled with sand. Let the muscles firm and flow downward around the bones.
9. Release and relax your arms to your side, feeling your breath come in and out.

BALANCING ON ONE LEG TO AWAKEN THE GLUTES

Even when new students are encouraged to use their gluteal muscles in the poses, some of them just won't be able to access them at first. When this happens, it may be due to a lack of exercise in general, or they may have developed a pattern of movement that doesn't include enough participation of the glutes. Working with poses where the students have to stand and balance on one leg encourages the glutes to work and reaps the most benefits. Though focusing on one-legged balance poses like Tree and Dancer while cueing the glutes is effective, flowing between one-legged poses brings an added challenge.

Before cueing students into Warrior 3 or other challenging one-legged postures, take a moment to practice Stork and ask them to stand on one foot while bringing the other knee up in front of them. Next, cue a few mini one-legged squats, which cannot be performed without the glutes helping. Keeping the knee on the standing leg a little bent at first helps many students to better feel the quadriceps and glutes working, and it also keeps them from just balancing on their bones or hyperextending their knee. Next ask them to extend one leg behind them, keeping the knee straight and the foot close to the floor, as if they were in ballet class. With the extended hip turned out slightly, cue a few gentle upward pulses with the leg. This practice should bring them into awareness of their glutes helping the hamstrings extend the leg and stabilize the pelvis. Finally, challenge the class to flow between these two positions, first Stork with the leg in front and then extending the same leg to the back to a modified Warrior 3 without letting the foot touch the ground. Over time as the students build strength, this can develop toward moving from Extended Hand-to-Big-Toe to a full Warrior 3.

Most students in public classes are open to a few moves that are not officially yoga if they understand what they are working towards. It only takes a moment out of a traditional yoga class to add these little mini one-legged squats and ballet pulses, but it will make a huge difference in students' progression into Warrior 3 and other challenging standing postures. Getting their glutes reactivated will also help them move more efficiently throughout their day.

Awakening Particularly Sleepy Glutes

When our glutes are engaging well and at the correct time in combination with other muscles, they help to extend and stabilize our hips.

However, our modern culture includes a lot of sitting during the day that contributes to weak, underachieving glutes. Low backs and hip flexors become tight from sitting, and the abdominals become weak.[1] Although the one-legged squat exercises described above — along with all the one-legged balances in yoga — are great for strengthening the glutes and the core, side-lying and prone exercises have been shown to be even more effective for getting the glutes to engage.[2] As yoga teachers, we can help ensure that students are indeed firing their glutes by infusing some non-weight bearing leg lifts into our beginning classes. An example would be lying prone in preparation for Locust and beginning by just lifting one leg and then the other. Taking a moment to experience these little leg lifts can give students the opportunity to feel their hamstrings and glutes working together to lift their leg. Another example is to combine side-lying leg lifts with Sleeping Vishnu (also known as Anantasana or Infinite pose), to recruit gluteus medius. For a complete side-lying flow that works both gluteus medius and the core, see the last practice in Chapter 6.

THE CHALLENGE OF TEACHING SEATED POSES

When it is time to go to the floor in yoga class and do seated poses, we often lose the attention of some new students. After all the talk and articles on the challenging standing poses and arm balances in the yoga feeds, very little is said about how hard it is to reach new students in the seated poses. So many people have been to fitness classes where there is some light, unengaged stretching at the end with little instruction, and so in their first yoga classes they assume it is the same thing. However, in yoga we want them to engage their muscles in these seated poses, firming their legs and using their core. Although some students are resistant to using their muscles and lengthening their back, these instructions protect the spine. Seated forward folds put pressure on the spine and can cause injuries over time (more detail on this topic will be covered in Chapter 7.) Let's look at Seated Forward Fold as an example of cueing deeper activation in the muscles while sitting.

Practice: Seated Forward Fold (For Students with Less Flexible Legs and Hips)

1. Sit with your legs in front of you in Staff. Place your feet about hip-distance apart. If this is uncomfortable or you have trouble sitting up straight, then sit on a folded yoga blanket or a larger yoga block.
2. Place your fingertips behind you on the floor to help you sit up as straight as possible. If you are sitting on a blanket or block, then you may also need to have blocks for your hands to rest on.
3. Imagine you are pressing the backs of your legs into the mat engaging your thighs and glutes. If you hyperextend, then keep your knees slightly bent and/or place a car wash sponge under your knees.
4. Imagine you are reaching your inner thighs towards the floor, gently firming them. Avoid letting your hips turn out with your feet and knees splaying out to the sides of the mat.
5. Imagine you have a resistance band around your thighs, and you are gently pressing your thighs away from each other into the band, firming your glutes.
6. Spread your toes out the best you can and pull your toes back towards you. Press forward a little with your big toe mounds and feel your arches engage and lift ("yoga toes").
7. Imagine the energy coming into your arches, up into your legs and into your pelvis.
8. Tone and lift the pit of your abdomen. Imagine a zipper moving from the pubic bone towards your belly button.
9. Elongate your spine, reaching the crown of your head higher.
10. Keep breathing into your ribs. Continue to firm your legs while you take a few deep breaths.
11. If you find you can sit up straight without your hands helping you, then take a strap and put it around your feet over your big toe mounds.
12. Hold one end of the strap in each hand and gently press the

big toe mounds into the strap. Keep your chest open and your shoulder blades on your back.

13. Keep your back elongated and resist the urge to round over.
14. Notice if there is any movement available to you in your hips. See if you can feel your hip pointers on the front of your pelvis move forward and down, folding forward over your thigh bones.
15. Your pelvis may not move very far forward. Just work on lengthening your spine and keeping your shoulder blades on your back.
16. To come out of the pose, keep your core engaged as you bring your hands behind you on the mat. Lean back on your hands to relax your core and back, let your legs relax, and take a few breaths.

Activating + Stabilizing

Activating the quadriceps and the glutes is a foundational element of yoga that requires frequent reminders to students, much like reminding them to breathe. Through creative cueing and sequencing, we can guide students to awaken and recruit these large muscles not just for practicing challenging asanas , but also for consistent, functional, and healthy movement. As we will discuss in Chapter 5, strengthening is the first priority over stretching.

5

STRETCHING THE HIPS CAREFULLY

Despite the growing interest in stabilizing and strengthening the body in the yoga culture, many communities continue the pursuit of extreme flexibility. Hypermobile, attractive models appear in ads selling magazines and products, while yoga teachers promote themselves on social media with poses that resemble gymnastics and circus work. Many of these popularly photographed poses involve extreme range of motion (ROM) in the hips. Since this is what students see, and it attracts them to yoga, it's difficult as a yoga teacher to undo that first impression. When this is combined with a "just do it" fitness attitude, students risk injuring their hips.

Yoga's huge popularity over the past few years has brought all shapes, sizes, and fitness levels into the practice. Students who are less flexible, whether naturally or due to sitting at their day jobs, are coming to yoga for relief from aches and pains. Doctors and physical therapists are referring people to yoga for stretching and relaxation. At the same time, yoga continues to attract people who are naturally flexible in their muscles and/or have hypermobile joints. In an attempt to quickly get into all the postures, flexible people try to become more flexible. This can bring imbalances throughout the body, particularly in the hip joints.

With these two extremes entering our classrooms at the same time, along with everyone in-between, we need a way to address these differences quickly without confusing the students. In this chapter, we will focus on specific cueing for the flexible and the not-so-flexible as we guide students safely into some of the most popular hip stretching poses.

While teaching hip stretches, I encourage all students to start slowly and get to know their limits by paying attention to how their body feels before going deeper into poses. I ask them to pay attention to any sensations in the joints and learn their natural boundaries first before trying to push to the edge. When teaching Pigeon or Cobbler to newer students, I like to compare learning the comfortable ROM of the hips with the way we learn the corners or perimeter of a car we haven't driven before. When we borrow a friend's car and we have to park it in a tight spot, we slow down. We don't know the exact perimeter of the car, so we proceed cautiously, maybe even backing up a little and readjusting. Once we get to know the car, we know we won't ding it and can pull right into a parking spot. It might take an afternoon to learn the perimeter of a friend's car, but it can take a few years to learn the limits of our own hips.

ABSOLUTE ROM DIFFERS IN INDIVIDUALS

Although we all have the same bones in our hips, their size, length, and angles vary. At the top of the femur (thigh bone), there is a neck with a head on it. The angle of that neck, called the femoral neck, can either reduce or increase the ROM.[1] How long or short, thin or thick this neck is also can affect the ROM. At some point, the neck comes into contact with the edge of the acetabulum (hip socket), and the student is then at bone-on-bone contact. Trying to push past this point can cause injury to the joint, particularly to the hip labrum.[2] Additionally, the location of the acetabulum varies, and this also affects the absolute ROM; it can be slightly higher, lower, forward, or more to the side, depending on the individual. **The takeaway here is**

that in the end, no matter how much a student stretches and works, there will be some poses they physically cannot achieve due to the structure of their bones.

Although this fact about the bones has become accepted by anatomy and therapy leaders in yoga, some teachers and students still operate under the idea that if they just work harder and stretch deeper they will be able to achieve any pose. Bony limitations exist though, and students will find this after they have practiced for a few years and seem to plateau in their flexibility. The challenge is to be able to discern the difference between the sensations of stretching tight muscles and the feeling of compression or "stuckness" that comes from the bones and joints.

Although it is popular with some yoga teachers to physically push on students' bodies to get them deeper into poses, I do not do this. I do not teach teachers to do it either. Light guiding touch for physical adjustments is fine when the student gives permission, but forcefully pushing on students is not a safe practice. If a student is in Cobbler and the teacher pushes down hard on their thighs in an attempt to get them deeper into the pose, they risk injuring the hip joint through bone-on-bone compression or attachment tears of the tendons and ligaments.

COBBLER

This classic pose is one most people have experienced before they ever show up at a yoga class. When I was a kid in the 1970's the gym teachers called it the Butterfly. The teacher would have us put the soles of our feet together and bounce our knees up and down like butterflies flying around. I still remember noticing that it didn't feel good to bounce my knees really hard, and so I would cheat and not really bounce (my inner yogi developing). As a kid, I was fast and strong but also so flexible that I would experience joint pain. I now know that all the running and cutting (changing directions quickly) in sports, without proper weight training and core integration, was just inflaming the joints of my mobile knees and hips.[3]

I've put on a lot of muscle since I started yoga, and this has reduced both the ROM in my hips and the pain and aches. However, I am still very careful in the "Butterfly" to engage my thighs and glutes and never force my knees to the ground. When I get to my end range of a forward fold, I include a subtle lift of my hip points and tone my deep belly. This keeps my pelvis from folding over to its absolute end ROM. Another way to explain this is that in order to stay out of my hip joints, I do a little rounding of my low back while in a deep forward fold. Let's look at some cueing for the flexible students like myself first, and then we can look at all the modifications that are needed for the rest — and the majority — of the students.

Practice: Cobbler for Very Flexible Students

1. From Staff, bring the soles of your feet together and place them in a comfortable position in front of you. Instead of pulling your feet in toward your pelvis, place your hands behind you and lift and shift your pelvis forward towards your feet.[4]
2. Ground your fingertips into the mat behind you for support as you elongate your spine.
3. Feel your low belly lifting in and up and your hip pointers drawing towards each other.
4. Breathe into your ribs, letting them expand.
5. Let the soles of your feet open up a little, like opening a book in front of you.
6. Press the sides of your feet into the mat and imagine you are drawing your feet away from each other, but you can't.
7. Feel your inner thighs and outer thighs firm up as you ground the sides of your feet into the mat while feeling your knees draw isometrically away from each other.
8. Continuing to keep the sides of your feet grounded, work your outer thighs gently downward while firming your glutes.

9. Keeping your back long, begin folding forward at your hips with your neck in line with your spine. Bring your hands in front of your shins on the mat for support as you fold forward.
10. If your torso folds down closely to your feet, then notice how the front of your hip joints feel. If you feel any compression or pinching at the front of your hips, then lift your hip pointers up slightly to round your low back some and create a little space in your hip joints.
11. Gently press your fingertips into the mat and draw them toward you, encouraging the elongation of your spine while pressing the feet down and out.
12. To come out of the pose, keep your low belly toned and use your fingertips on the mat for support as you come upright. Once sitting up straight, place a hand behind each of your thighs to help bring your thighs up, stretching your legs out one at a time and returning to Staff.

WORKING WITH LESS FLEXIBLE STUDENTS

When I start to teach Cobbler, I often see pained expressions on a number of students' faces. In an attempt to practice the pose, their backs round, and their knees are higher than their pelvis. Since many people sit all day at their office jobs, their hips become tight and sore, so starting with seated poses often makes them uncomfortable. In this case, it is better to start class lying on the back or standing. After the warm-up, move into standing poses first to warm the legs, hips, and back. If we wait until after the standing work to practice seated poses, then it will be safer and more tolerable for many students.

Even after warming up, many of the less flexible students will still need props for support. To reduce the flexion of the hips we can offer a blanket or block to sit on. In some cases, a student might prefer sitting with their back against a wall for support. For the knees, we can suggest they place a block under their thighs. At first there may be a resistance to putting the blocks under the thighs, as they think that will reduce the stretch. But the opposite is true, because when we support the thighs, the adductors (inner thigh muscles) will stop gripping and begin to release. Over time, as the body opens up, the blocks can be replaced with blankets or big car wash sponges.

As students are learning this posture, encourage them to be gentle with their feet and ankles. Pulling or forcing the feet in toward the groins can cause the inner thighs and groins to tighten and also puts the knees at risk. In the practice above, we asked students to move their pelvis toward their feet instead of grasping the feet and drawing them in. This can reduce torque on the knees. With the less flexible student, this move is even more important to offer, as it often reduces tension in the adductors and hips.

Those with less flexible hips enjoy supported Cobbler with a blanket under the pelvis and blocks under the legs.

Practice: Cobbler for Less Flexible Students

1. Sit with your legs out long in front of you in Staff, and place a folded blanket under your knees.
2. Bring your hands behind you and come on to your fingertips, sitting up as straight as you can.
3. Keeping your feet in front of the blanket, bend your knees and bring the soles of the feet together. Using your grounded fingers or hands lift and shift your pelvis toward your feet and onto the blanket.
4. If your knees are higher than the top of your hips (iliac crest), then place blocks under your thighs to support them.
5. Continue to keep your fingers planted behind you for support; avoid rounding over. Use blocks under your fingertips if needed.
6. Draw your low belly in and up while imagining you are lifting your ribs up off of your hips.
7. Widen through the collar bones and let your head float right above the spine.
8. Press the sides of your feet into the mat and work them away from each other isometrically, firming the inner and outer thighs.
9. Breathe into your ribs, letting them widen to both sides. Lift your hands off the floor or blocks for a moment and see if you can continue to sit up straight without support. If you can't, then put your fingers back down behind you and continue to work on elongating your spine.
10. If you can sit without support, then bring your hands to each side of you, or right in front, and work on hinging a little at the hips.
11. If you are comfortable with your fingers out in front of you, then press your fingertips into the mat and isometrically draw them back towards you to help elongate your upper back.
12. As you fold forward, focus on keeping a long spine and avoid rounding over.

13. To come out of the pose, use your hands to support your thighs one at a time while lifting your knees up and stretching your legs out in front of you and returning to Staff. Bring your hands behind you as you lean back, relax, and breathe.

STANDING WIDE-LEGGED FORWARD BEND

Standing Wide-Legged Forward Bend is another popular hip opening pose, and the cueing needed for mixed level classes is also very different depending on the students. Sometimes I wish we could separate students into classes depending on their hip ROM and movement patterns, but in the real world we have to be prepared for anyone to walk into the classroom. Many of my male students struggle to get comfortable in Wide-Legged Forward Bend due to tight hips and hamstrings. The pelvic floor is often tighter in men than women, and this adds to the lower degree of ROM for the hips.[5] On the other extreme, there are very flexible women who have no problem getting their heads on the floor in this position. These flexible students risk injuring their hamstring attachments by hanging in the forward bend without muscular support. Let's take a look at cueing for both of these extremes and then how we can try to fuse them together in a class.

Practice: Standing Wide-Legged Forward Bend for Less Flexible Students

1. Take a wide stance while facing the long side of your mat. Make sure the distance of the stance is comfortable for your hips, knees, and ankles. Place two blocks in front of you, shoulder-width apart.
2. Let your knees and toes track together, pointing as forward as you can comfortably. If the knees, ankles, or hips are uncomfortable, then turn your hips out slightly, letting the knees and toes follow the turn-out.
3. Make sure you have equal weight on both feet while pressing into the big toe mounds and the outer heels of both feet.

4. Zip your belly up from your pubic bone to your belly button, keeping your low belly toned.
5. Breathe into your ribs smoothly and evenly.
6. Put your hands on your hips, bend your knees, and float your heels slightly off the floor.
7. Fold forward at the hips, and then put your hands on the blocks.
8. With the knees still bent, ground the heels and elongate your spine by reaching the crown of your head and the base of your spine in opposite directions.
9. Imagine you have a resistance band around your thighs and you are working your legs away from each other into the band.
10. Imagine you are lifting up your inner ankles towards your groins, feeling engagement and energy moving up your inner legs into your thighs and belly.
11. Continue to keep your knees bent and your hands on the blocks, and draw your belly in and up to work on creating a natural curve in your lumbar spine.
12. To come out of the pose, keep your knees bent and put your hands on your hips. While coming up, keep a long back and isometrically work your legs away from each other, as if you have a resistance band around them.

Students with less flexible hips and hamstrings are more comfortable in Wide-Legged Forward Bend with blocks under the hands. Focus on elongating the spine.

Practice: Standing Wide-Legged Forward Bend for Flexible Students

1. Take a wide stance while facing the long side of your mat. Make sure the distance of the stance is comfortable for your ankles and hips, backing off some from your absolute ROM.
2. Keep your hips in a neutral position, neither turning in (medially rotating) nor turning out (laterally rotating). Let your knees and toes follow your hips, pointing as forward as is comfortable.
3. Keep equal weight on both feet, pressing actively into the big toe mounds and outer heels.
4. Tone your low belly, lifting the pit of the abdomen in and up.
5. Imagine you have a resistance band around your thighs, and you are working your legs away from each other into the band, activating your thighs and glutes.

6. Put your hands on your hips and fold forward at the hips, and then place your hands on the mat.
7. If you can easily get your head on the floor, narrow your stance enough to get your head off of the floor so you can elongate your spine.
8. Firm the muscles around the sit bones and imagine that there is an energetic connection between the sit bones and the heels, subtly grounding the sit bones towards the heels.
9. Imagine you are lifting your inner ankles up towards your groins, feeling the inner thighs firm.
10. Continue breathing into your ribs while you work to hold these engagements in this pose. To come out of the pose, isometrically work your legs away from each other as you bring your torso up.

Working with Differences

When we have both extremes in the same class, we can focus first on the cues that will work fine for both types, and then add in a few options. Lifting the heels up, and then forward folding while balancing on the big toe mounds is a fun option that works for everyone. It also helps to soften the upper hamstrings just below the sit bones and will allow the tighter student to fold at the hips more deeply.[6] Balancing on the toes doesn't hurt the flexible student, and in order to stay balanced folding over, they will have to engage their muscles. This may also encourage a more engaged core and avoid too much arching of the back as they fold forward. Abducting the hips in the pose energizes the quadriceps and glutes for both extremes, and additional cues can be added to encourage engagement such as "press your feet away from each other" or "imagine you are trying to make your mat longer." Once the students are in the pose, we can quickly add a few extra cues such as "if you are less flexible, keep your knees bent and put your hands on blocks," or "if you are very flexible, remember to tone the muscles around your sit bones, and ground your sit bones towards your heels." With experienced students, it's nice to add extra little cues to deepen the experience like "lift your inner ankles up towards your groins."

No matter the student's body type, many beginners struggle to stabilize their pelvis when attempting side-to-side or revolved variations of Wide-Legged Forward Fold. Keeping equal weight on both feet and actively pressing the big toe mounds and the outer heels helps students stay stable as they walk their fingers toward one foot and then the other. In Revolved Wide-Legged Forward Fold, some students may need to let their hips follow the twist a little for comfort and safety in the SI joints. With a mixed group, I focus on cueing core engagement and twisting through the ribs with equal weight on both feet rather than a perfectly level pelvis.

Students who are less flexible tend to turn their hips out, and their knees and toes follow the turn-out, while very flexible students let their hips rotate inward with the knees and toes pointing inward toward the midline. It was popular years ago to tell all students to medially rotate the hips in this pose. Everyone was asked to stand a little "pigeon toed" with the idea of getting the inner thighs to move back and the sit bones to move up and away. This ended up giving many yoga practitioners hamstring attachment injuries, and for those who were less flexible, it added torque to the knees. To reduce injuries, teach from the hips first, and encourage students to keep their hips as neutral as is comfortable for them with their knees and toes in alignment. For less flexible students, we must keep in mind that they may have to be slightly turned out with the feet also turned out in order to keep the knees happy.

PIGEON

The hip stretching Pigeon is the subject of many yoga articles, blogs, and social media posts. Although it is popular and can be therapeutic, it can also cause discomfort and injuries to the knees and low back when careful alignment is not used. The hips and back can also be at risk when students try to move too fast into the more advanced King

Pigeon and other variations like Mermaid. Students seem to either love or hate Pigeon, and in a mixed class we've got to be ready with a number of modifications to keep everyone's hips and knees happy and healthy.

The question of where to place the front shin in Pigeon continues to create disputes among teachers, and although we might want to avoid the conflict, it's important to address it and give students options. After asking what students are feeling in the pose, we can cue accordingly. We want to avoid any pressure or pain in the knee. Traditionally, the front shin was placed parallel to the front of the mat, often in an attempt to deepen the pose. For many people, this can create a torque in their knee. In order to safely have the shin parallel with the front of the mat, the student must have an ability to deeply rotate their hip laterally (turned out). Otherwise, the force of pressing the shin down along with the pelvis goes right into the knee.

Some students are more comfortable with a block under their hip in Pigeon.

I experienced knee pain myself many years ago when teachers would try to correct my alignment by asking me to put my shin parallel to the front of the mat. Although I have reasonably open and flexible hips, if I put my shin parallel with the mat it doesn't work for my knees. In order to keep my knees happy, I keep the shin in front of me pointing towards the opposite hip. For example, if my right knee is forward, then my right heel is near my left hip pointer. I let the calf of the right leg roll up a bit so that the sole of my foot is angling upward. My intention with this alignment is to keep my thigh bone (femur) and my shin bone (tibia) in alignment with each other. I don't want my shin bone going in one direction and my thigh bone in another, or my knee is torqued.

Some students with the ability to deeply rotate the hip laterally can indeed keep their shin parallel to the mat, but these students are rare. For beginning classes, it is best to show the heel near the opposite hip pointer option to avoid students hurting their knees while they learn the practice. Due to the fact that students' bodies are different, we have to leave room for there to be a number of "right" ways to do this pose.

The front shin dispute often leads to the front foot dispute. For years many instructors have taught students to flex the front ankle, along with the shin being parallel with the mat. The thinking behind this cue is that if the ankle is flexed, then the muscles along the front of the shin will engage more deeply, stabilizing and protecting the knee. Certainly, engagement of our muscles in the poses protects our joints in general, but if the student is torquing their knee in the attempt to get deeper in this pose, a flexed foot won't help. The best position for the foot and ankle will vary depending on the individual's knees and hips and where they feel most comfortable placing the foot. I prefer doing my yoga toes with my ankle only slightly flexed. For other students, the hard flex of the ankle works best. The intention behind this choice is the same as the discussion above with the shin. We want to keep the bones aligned and avoid twisting or torquing the knee.

Practice: Basic Pigeon

1. Start on your hands and knees in Table and shift your torso forward as you slide your right knee up toward your right hand. Your right foot will rest on the mat near your left hip pointer (ASIS).
2. Leaving your right foot on the mat, let the sole of the foot turn up slightly. Extend your right toes (they will be pressing into the mat some) to help engage your arch.
3. Curl your back left toes under and walk your foot backwards as your pelvis drops down towards the mat.
4. If you struggle to get your pelvis to the floor, then put a blanket or a block under your right buttock.
5. Level your pelvis out the best you can, making sure one hip isn't higher than the other.
6. Place your hands about shoulder-width apart on the mat on either side of your front knee.
7. Engage the thighs and firm the glutes. Press your legs into the mat and work them gently away from each other as if you are trying to make your mat a little wider.
8. Lift the low belly in and up while imagining you are squeezing your hip pointers (ASIS) towards each other.
9. Now point your left toes, and press the top of the left foot into the mat like you are pressing on a button.
10. You have the option of bringing your forearms to the floor in front of you to deepen the pose in the right hip.
11. If you want to come a little deeper into a backbend, first tone your upper abdominals by imagining you are reaching your bottom ribs towards your hips, then come up onto your hands if you were on your forearms, and lift your heart, letting your head follow.
12. As the pose develops remember to keep firming the thighs and glutes, engaging the core and breathing into the ribs.
13. To come out of the pose, keep your muscles firm. Press into

your hands to lift your torso up, and then shift back into Table.

Pigeon Modifications for Those with Knee Problems and Less Flexible Hips

I've had students of all ages complain about their knees and hips as they attempt Pigeon. The tendency with less flexible students is to lean their pelvis over to one side to get to the floor to take the tension off of the hips and the hip flexor. These students need a blanket, block, or flat bolster under the hip of the bent knee to help level the hips and reduce the tension on the front knee. In addition, it may be better for them to walk their hands forward of the front knee or come down on their forearms. Coming down onto the forearms takes the tension and pinching out of the low back, but it can add too much discomfort to the hip with the knee in front. An in-between option is to have the student put their forearms on blocks in front of them, reminding them to keep their elbows under their shoulders for the most support. If none of these options work, then some students need to practice this pose on their backs.

To help students who find Pigeon a challenge, place a car wash sponge under the low back and use a strap around the thigh.

Practice: Modified Pigeon on the Back with a Big Car Wash Sponge

1. Lie on your back with your feet on the ground and your knees bent.
2. Press into your feet, lift your pelvis up, and place a big sponge under your lumbar curve.
3. Lie on the sponge and take a moment to feel your lumbar curve.
4. Cross your left ankle over just past your right thigh, and place your hands around your right thigh.
5. Before pulling your right thigh in towards your chest, notice if you have completely smashed the sponge. Has your tailbone and lower pelvis started to curl off the ground? If so, then release your lower pelvis back onto the mat and try to find at least a little curve in your lumbar, so there is just a little squish in your sponge.
6. If you find that you can't keep a natural curve in your lumbar spine, then place a strap folded in half around your right thigh and hold the ends of the strap, reducing the flexion of your hip.
7. Pay attention to how your left knee feels and adjust your left ankle up or down on your right thigh for comfort. If there is any tension or feeling of torque in the left knee, then back off some until the knee is happy. If you are using a strap, then let it out some until the knee is comfortable.
8. Firm both thighs and draw your hip pointers towards each other, toning the low belly.
9. Keep the shoulders quiet and grounded on the mat, and relax your jaw and neck.
10. Slowly draw your right thigh closer in if you can, keeping it tracking so that the right knee stays in line with your right shoulder.
11. Once your thigh is as close as it can be comfortably, you have the option to straighten your right leg as much as you easily

can. Work your "yoga toes" by flexing your right ankle and gently spreading the toes.

12. Firm up your right thigh, and again check that your pelvis is still grounded.
13. To come out of the pose, bend your right leg, and while keeping your core engaged, place your right foot back on the mat. Return your left foot to the floor also, and take a moment to breathe while keeping your knees bent to let your back and hips release.

SCIATICA AND PIGEON

What do we do with a student who comes into class wanting to learn Pigeon for their sciatica? First and foremost, yoga teachers do not give out medical advice. What we can say is that sometimes yoga helps sciatica, and sometimes it doesn't. It depends on what is causing the sciatica, or what the student thinks is sciatica, and they need a medical evaluation to make that determination.

Students come and ask about this after googling "how to help my sciatica" and finding articles showing various yoga stretches, including Pigeon. Versions of piriformis stretches, including variations of Pigeon, are indeed used in physical therapy for sciatica. These stretches are used when the doctor or physical therapist determines the piriformis muscle is tight and is the source of the pain due to compression of the sciatic nerve. However, a tight piriformis is not the only reason someone can have sciatica. It can sometimes be caused by nerve compression, pinching, or damage in the low back. In some cases, the nerve problems can make the piriformis spasm, which causes shooting pain down the leg, and in these cases it may have nothing to do with the muscle being tight or weak. For this reason, if a student comes to my class who has diagnosed themselves with sciatica, and they don't feel better within a few months of yoga practice, I will strongly encourage them to see their doctor. I'll take a moment to explain that yoga isn't the cure-all for sciatica. All that said, I have seen some students become pain free after attending a few months of classes, and that is amazing when it happens.

HYPERMOBILITY

As we mentioned in the beginning of this chapter, the risk for hip injury increases for hypermobile students when they push to the limits of their ROM. Some of these students try to go deeper and deeper just to feel a stretch. They complain in class that they don't feel anything as they relax into full Pigeon. Note that there is a difference between the terms "flexible" and "hypermobile." A person can have naturally flexible muscles, but in a smaller percentage of cases the mobility is actually coming from the joints, and this is called hypermobility. Hypermobility is related to lax ligaments in the joints, and stretching joints that are already lax only makes them less stable. In some cases, these same students may have some tight muscles that are working to stabilize the hypermobile joint.

The best yoga practice for these students is one that focuses on strengthening the muscles, but this can be a hard sell if they are interested in working towards the poses they see on Instagram. However, if they are interested in getting stronger and reducing joint pain, then a slow, gentle, strengthening practice may help them, as it has me.

Whether the student is hypermobile in their joints or generally flexible in their muscles, as their teacher I make sure they understand the risks of attempting the poses that require a high ROM in the hips. Although I know yogis who for the last 30 years have practiced extreme postures while also maintaining the integrity of their joints, I also know some who have damaged their hips. Hip replacements and surgeries are not rare in older yogis — it's just not talked about much publicly. Damaging the hip labrum (ring of cartilage) is a common injury in ballet, where extreme external rotation is required, and I've met yogis who have had this same injury and have required the same surgery. The main difference between the students who hurt themselves and the ones who don't likely has more to do with how they are built, and whether they have sought out a knowledgeable teacher. Getting into poses requiring extreme ROM, even for the students who are built to do them, requires specific and careful sequencing to warm and open the body. Exactly what sequencing is needed, and how many repetitions, varies between students. Having a skilled teacher who is experienced with these types of postures, and who can observe the body and see where the tightness, mobility, and/or energetic blocks are, makes all the difference. An experienced teacher also knows when to tell a student to back off.

Creative Cueing + Options

Whether our students want to work toward acrobatic poses or prefer a more gentle, supported practice, we can encourage them to learn the possibilities and the limits for their own hips and bodies. Even with their differences, we can help all of our students by offering modifications and options. Despite yoga's capacity for healing and health, injuries do occur, especially when students push themselves too deeply and too fast. As teachers, we can create a safer environment for our students to explore and learn the practice by creating a relaxed atmosphere and using a variety of cues for different body types.

6
AWAKENING THE CORE AND STABILIZING THE PELVIS

Whenever yoga teachers gather and someone brings up abdominal exercises, an old and continuing debate begins again. There are many different views on which exercises work the core best and in the safest way possible. The debate doesn't stop with yoga teachers but also arises between fitness instructors. The truth is that abdominal exercises sell well to the public, because many people want a flatter, stronger looking stomach! Teachers try to sell their own "amazing core workout" to create those perfect abs and compete with each other, fueling the debate. Even within the world of physical therapy, I've heard various theories as to how to properly awaken and work the core muscles. Years ago when I couldn't stop asking questions about abdominals at a workshop, a friend told me, "be careful Becca, you might start a bar fight in here." I didn't get what he was saying at the time, but now I do. In hindsight, it was a great joke that took me about 8 years to get. This chapter covers my current views on the core and how to guide students into core awareness and engagement while creating smooth, efficient movement and stability.

So what is this elusive core that instructors talk about? Do students even know what we mean when we say the word "core"? In yoga and fitness classes, students often hear, "pull in your core," or "tighten your core" or "pull your belly button to your spine." Some teachers also like to use the traditional yoga terms that refer to the core, including Mula Bandha (a focal point for lifting the pelvic floor) and Uddiyana Bandha (a focal point in the low belly, below the belly button, that we draw in and up to engage the abdominals). Early on when I first attended yoga workshops, I remember hearing a teacher shouting, "Mula Bandha, Mula Bandha!" I had no idea at the time what he meant and started giggling. I believe the first time a student hears one of these cues or terms, they either ignore it and keep going, or they make a decision as to what it means to them. The understanding stops there unless the teacher's cues change. Many students will just pull in their stomach around their belly button and never get any deeper into their body or awareness.

Some students who have been leading sedentary lives have lost strength in their abdominals, or they've lost the ability or awareness to recruit them at the right time. When they first join yoga class, many students will compensate for weak abdominals by using other muscles instead. A person can do a lot of yoga with their larger surface muscles, and they may even look good in pictures of the poses. When we watch them move though, their lack of core integration and pelvic stability becomes apparent. A few indicators for a lack of deep core stability are trouble balancing on one leg, stability problems in the opposite arm/leg balance variations (Bird Dog), and overusing the low back muscles in many poses.

By using different cues, we help people break their old habits and help them integrate all of the deep core muscles into their asana and daily movements. The deepest core muscles are designed to work behind the scenes whenever we move. After they are awakened and working, the imagery may not be as important, as the body remembers how to move properly with practice.

WHY NOT USE THE CLASSIC "BELLY BUTTON TO SPINE" CUE?

There are a number of reasons this classic cue is not very effective. The first is that when students hear "pull in your stomach" most of them will just engage their rectus abdominis (RA) to draw the belly button in without using the rest of their abdominals. The RA runs down the center front of the torso, and it works to flex the lumbar spine. Although it is important, and many fitness enthusiasts like to work it for the 6-pack look, it is the most surface of our abdominal muscles and can't stabilize the torso by itself. We need to work all the deeper muscles as discussed above.

The second reason not to use this classic cue is when most students pull their belly button to their spine, they also tuck their tailbone under, which creates a little posterior pelvic tilt. This happens because the belly button cue activates the RA, and the RA flexes (rounds) the lumbar, and this is often accompanied by the engagement of the gluteus maximus (the largest buttocks muscle), which squeezes and clenches inward. All of these actions cause the students to put more pressure on their low backs while also hardening the front of the hip flexors. There are only a few poses, like Crow or Half Boat, where a posterior tilt would be helpful (more explanation about the terminology on pelvic positions will come later in this chapter).

Thirdly, whenever we do abdominal work, we want to try to limit the pressure we are putting on the pelvic floor. When we deeply draw in the belly button all the tissue and fluid in the belly has to go either above or below the cinch created at the belly button. Take a moment to deeply draw your belly button in towards your spine and see if you feel any pressure on your pelvic floor. Even if you can't feel it yet, there is abdominal pressure on your pelvic floor that can cause dysfunction over time. Another way to explain this concept is to think about what happens when you squeeze a tube of toothpaste right in the middle. The paste moves to either end of the tube, separated by the pinch. If you put enough pressure on it, paste will start to come out on the end of the tube that isn't sealed. If we take this concept back to our bodies, the pressure will be focused on the pelvic floor. When practicing classic abdominal exercises, we need to work on reducing the pressure below. One way to approach this is to try and keep some room for our organs to move upward within our rib cage as we curl, by keeping our ribs open and as wide as possible, rather than letting them clamp down on our torso. This action creates a feeling of the abdominals sliding up under the rib cage.

Core Muscle Review

Let's quickly review some aspects of our core muscles. Our abdominal muscles include the rectus abdominis (the 6-pack muscle, RA for short), and the internal and external obliques. The deepest abdominal muscles are the transverse abdominals (TA for short). Also included in the core are the tiny multifidi, the deepest muscles that run all along the spine from the sacrum up to the top of the neck. The pelvic floor is also often included in most descriptions of the core. In traditional Pilates, they refer to the deepest core muscles as the "inner unit" or the "powerhouse," and they include the TA, pelvic floor, multifidi, and diaphragm.[1] In summary, it's not just the 6-pack muscle that we are interested in awakening and strengthening, it is all the muscles that work together as the core unit. Whenever we move, the TA, the pelvic floor, and the multifidi automatically work together deep within the body to create balance and stability.

When people start to develop movement and pain issues, it can sometimes be traced to these inner muscles not working well together. When we sit as much as we do in modern life, the core doesn't get enough use to stay strong and healthy. In some cases, the multifidi stop working as well as they need to and this creates back pain.[2] If the timing is off in this inner system, this can also cause problems as other muscles try to do the work of the core. Although not as common, people can also develop movement and pain issues when they work the core too much. Tightness in the pelvis and the pelvic floor, along with repeated downward pressure, can cause a variety of problems. Moving and walking is a positive step toward healing the body, as the inner unit does awaken in many people with just consistent daily movement. As yoga teachers, we can jump start this progress to better health by using imagery to help the process of first awakening and integrating the core into asana, and then daily movement.

BONE CUES FOR THE PELVIS

Of all the different imagery cues in yoga, I feel like the ones around the pelvis and the core can be the most effective at quickly getting people deeper into the body and more stable. I try to include the word "imagine" in the cueing to help people realize that what I'm asking is not so literal, like lifting a foot off of the floor. With the cues below, we are guiding students to feel the energetic connections between two bone points.

In order to effectively teach these cues, we must first help the students learn several bony landmarks. It's not hard at all to convey these to even the newest student. Once every few months in my public classes, I quickly repeat where these landmarks are so that new people can work their way into my classes.

Let's review them before we start using them for imagery.

Practice: Finding the Bony Landmarks of the Pelvis.

1. Stand in Mountain with your hands resting on your hips, thumbs towards the back and fingers at the front.
2. With your fingers find your hip pointers on the front of your pelvis below your waist. These are called the anterior superior iliac spine (ASIS).
3. With your thumbs find the bony points on the back of your pelvis below your waist. They are near where you can see dimples on the back of your pelvis, much closer together than

the ASIS. These points are called the posterior superior iliac spine (PSIS).

4. The pubic bone is on the front of your pelvis below your belly button at the bottom center.
5. The sacrum is on the back of your pelvis in the middle. To find it place your palm on the back of your pelvis in the middle and feel the large flat bone.
6. Your tail bone is at the end of your sacrum and is called the coccyx.
7. The bones that you sit on at the bottom of your pelvis are called ischial tuberosities, commonly referred to as your sit bones.

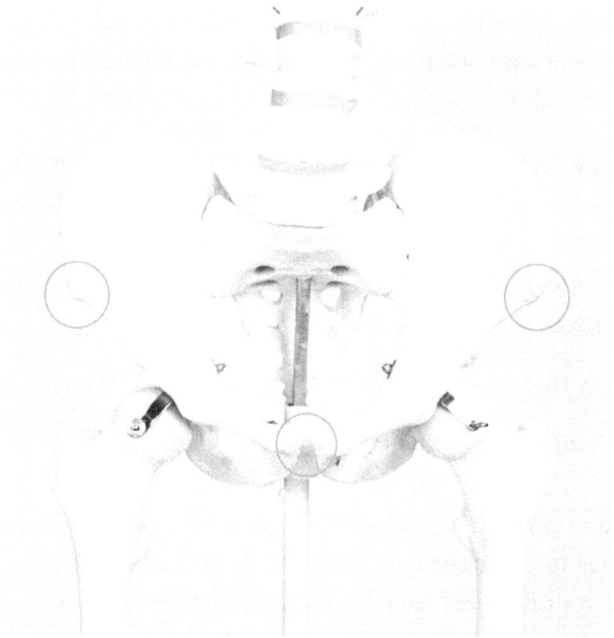

The circles on either side of the pelvis show the location of the anterior superior iliac spine (ASIS). The small circle in the lower middle shows the location of the pubic symphysis. The bones that come together here are usually referred to as the pubic bone.

Bone Cue Basics

We can use these bony landmarks to cue asana in many creative ways. The following list covers some basic examples of the movement we are encouraging in the core. Give each one a try and see what you find.

1. Imagine you have a zipper from your pubic bone to your belly button.
2. Imagine you are drawing your hip pointers towards each other.
3. Imagine you are drawing your PSIS towards each other.
4. Imagine you are lifting a point at the middle of the sacrum up your spine.

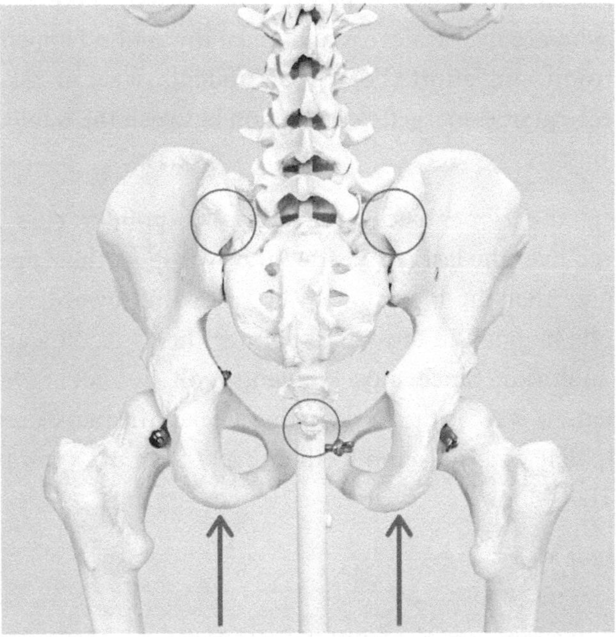

The circles on either side of the back of the pelvis show the location of the posterior superior iliac spine (PSIS). The sacrum is below these two points in the center. The smaller circle near the bottom of the pelvis shows the location of they coccyx (tailbone). The arrows at the bottom show the location of the sit bones.

These basic cues can be combined with other imagery in an attempt to reach students. An example: "imagine you are putting on your tight jeans fresh from the dryer, zipping them up from public bone to belly button." Let's take a closer look at the classic zipper cue.

Combining Zipper Cues with Bony Landmarks

A common imagery cue that goes back many years is imagining zippers[3] in certain places on the body to help engage muscles and gather energy. Asking students to imagine they are zipping up a zipper that starts at the pubic bone and goes up to the navel is an effective cue. The zipper cue can be extended up the front of the body along the midline to the xiphoid process (base of the sternum) to help those students who have a tendency to pop their ribs out. Holding too tightly above the belly button can get in the way of breathing if they make the "zipper" too tight. Whatever cue we give, there will be a few students who are overachievers and make the action happen with too much tension and effort. For those students we can ask them to instead feel a gentle energetic connection between the pubic bone and the belly button.

Combining the zipper cues with bony hip pointer cues has been popularized over the last few years. After we zip up the zipper, we can also imagine that the hip pointers are drawing towards each other. Just a gentle hugging in of the hip pointers helps to activate the deep TA and multifidi. Since most students will not identify with the muscle names, we can just ask if they feel a firmness occurring in their belly that wraps around to their back. Let's try a few bone cues with the Half Moon.

Practice: Half Moon

1. Place two blocks at the front of your mat.
2. Starting in Mountain, spread your toes and ground down, connecting with your feet.
3. Draw your hip pointers towards each other and zip your belly up from pubic bone to belly button.

4. Keeping the connection to your core, fold forward while keeping a long spine, and place your hands on the blocks.
5. Shift your weight into the left foot, pressing evenly into the big toe mound and the outer heel.
6. Bend your left knee a little, feeling the thigh and glutes firm.
7. Take an inhale to prepare, and on the exhale lift up your right leg behind you to about hip height, keeping the knee straight.
8. Firm your right thigh and flex your right foot.
9. Hug the hip pointers towards each other, again reconnecting with your core. Then, begin to lift your right hip up towards the ceiling. There is no need to "stack" the hips here. Just lift the right hip up until you find a comfortable spot.
10. As your right hip lifts up, let your knees and toes naturally follow in line with your hip. Try not to turn out your hip and leg like a dancer.
11. If you feel balanced, then you can bring your right hand off of the block and place it on your right hip.
12. If you feel a pinching in your low back or SI joints, then lower your right hip back down a little until your back is comfortable.
13. Lengthen your spine while imagining that you are trying to float your ribs away from your hips, making your side waists feel longer.
14. If you want to start to work towards looking to the side or above, then first begin to work on rotating your ribs gently towards the ceiling: keep your hips just as they are, and rotate just your ribs upward, letting your gaze follow.
15. To come out, take an inhale to prepare. On the exhale, place your right hand back on the block and then bring your right foot to the floor. Press evenly into your feet, bringing hands to your hips and then return to Mountain.

Cues for Finding the Core from the PSIS

Another way to access and connect with the deep core muscles is to start initiating movement and awareness from the back of the pelvis near the PSIS points. Asking students to imagine they are gently bringing their PSIS towards each other often gets a similar engagement and reaction as the hip pointer cue. Some students struggle to connect with the back body, so I always try the ASIS points first. That said, I've introduced this concept to beginners, and a large number of them began sweating while holding Tree (or another standing balance pose) using this imagery. When students suddenly feel warm, like a mini hot flash, or begin to sweat when holding a pose, this indicates that they are connecting and working with their deepest abdominals. I first experienced this myself in Pilates and then was able to connect with the same experience holding yoga poses. If you are integrated with your deep core in the poses, you won't need external heat to warm the muscles. The heat will build up inside you.

Once I feel students are connecting with the PSIS and ASIS cues, I like to encourage them to try and feel the experience of circling energy between the front and back body. When we squeeze the ASIS together, the energy wraps towards the front body, and when we squeeze the PSIS together, the energy wraps towards the back body. Next, I'll begin adding other imagery beyond the basic bone cues that helps to deepen the experience, and also to hopefully reach those students that find the bone cues confusing.

One of the images I like to use is drawstring yoga pants, although it takes a little explaining. I have students imagine they have a pair of low-rise yoga pants with a drawstring that they have put on backwards. Sitting cross legged, I ask them to lean forward a little and imagine they are pulling the drawstrings to gather the pants. Then I ask them to tie the drawstrings in a bow at the back of their pelvis. The drawstring image will hopefully bring a feeling of firmness around the front of the body and then a feeling of energy wrapping around to the back body.

Practice: Opposite Arm and Leg Balance (Bird Dog)

1. Come to your hands and knees with your hands a little in front of your shoulders and your knees under your hips.
2. Imagine your drawstring pants are on backwards, and pull the strings gently up, gathering the cord around your low waist. Then tie the cord into a bow right below your waist.
3. Stay with the feeling of the drawstring firming and stabilizing, and also gently zip up the low belly from pubic bone to belly button.
4. Take your right foot back, straightening your right leg with your toes turned under on the mat.
5. Imagine you are trying to lift your right leg up but you can't.
6. Feel your right thigh and buttock firm and connect with your belly. Then lift the right leg up parallel to the floor while keeping the thigh firm and the foot flexed.
7. Work to keep your pelvis level and your neck in line with your spine.
8. Lengthen your spine, reaching the crown of your head one way and your pelvis in the opposite direction.
9. Imagine you are trying to lift your left palm off the floor but you can't. Feel the muscles around your shoulder blade firm.
10. Now lift your left hand off the floor and then stretch your left arm out parallel to the floor, palm facing the midline.
11. To add some movement to this pose, keep your spine long as you move your right knee directly under your right hip, then begin to round your back while bringing your right knee towards your left elbow and your elbow towards your knee.
12. In order to bring this action a little deeper into your core, try gently hugging your hand on the floor (right hand) towards your knee on the floor (left knee) as you round your back. You may feel energy moving into the pelvis and belly.
13. Inhale as you move back out to the opposite arm/leg balance, and even take a small backbend, lifting the right leg and left arm a little above you.

14. Repeat steps 11 through 13 a few more times. When you are done, place your hands and knees on the mat and shift back into Pose of the Child.

CONNECTING TO THE CORE THROUGH THE SACRUM

Our sacrum is the large triangular bone on the back of our pelvis, and we can find it in between the PSIS points. The bone's flat surface covers the middle of the back of the pelvis. We can cue a feeling of lifting up from this area similar to the language we used with the PSIS points. This helps to engage the small deep multifidi muscles that help to stabilize our pelvis and low back along with the TA and pelvic floor. Using elevator imagery, we can combine the feeling of these muscles drawing together and lifting up. An example is, "Imagine you have elevator doors on the back of your pelvis, close the doors and now draw the elevator up to the next floor." This popular Pilates cue works well with students who connect quickly with imagery, but for others it's a mystery. Another cue I've been experimenting with involves finding a point in the middle of the sacrum and then another point on the front of the pelvis at a corresponding height. The point on the front body is around 2 inches above the pubic bone. I ask students to draw those two points towards each other creating an energetic connection between them, and then lift them both up. Once they understand the cue, I shorten it to, "plug it in, lift it up." Let's try applying this idea in Big Toe Hold.

Practice: Modified Big Toe Hold

1. Stand in Mountain with your right side facing the wall and place your right palm on the wall. Stand far enough away from the wall so that your elbow can be bent some and your right shoulder is comfortable.
2. Become aware of your breath moving your ribs.
3. Shift your weight onto your right foot.

4. Bend your left knee and place your left big toe just behind you like a little kick stand as you find your balance.
5. Find a point on the middle of your sacrum and another corresponding point on your low belly and draw these two points towards each other, and then lift them up together.
6. Press actively into your outer right heel and big toe mound as you lift your left knee in front of you and a little above your left hip.
7. Clasp your fingers around your left shin, just below the knee.
8. If you struggle holding the balance, then use your left hand on your shin and keep your right hand on the wall as you gain strength. If you are not struggling to balance, then see if you can bring your right hand to your right hip.
9. Level your hips, making sure that you didn't lift up your left hip along with your left leg.
10. Feel your spine lengthen as you reach the crown of your head up.
11. Let your sit bones feel a little heavy as they connect energetically with your heels.
12. Reestablish the connection to your core as you "plug it in and lift it up." See if you can feel the energy rising from your pelvic floor all the way up to your throat.
13. Let your shoulders gently hug your torso softening around the feeling of your inner core lifting in and up.
14. Keep your collarbones wide and your jaw relaxed.
15. Keeping your left knee bent, challenge your balance by moving your left knee out to the side while still maintaining your elongated spine and core awareness. If you struggle to stay stable, then hold onto your knee with your left hand as you take it out to the side.
16. Keeping your core lifted and your thighs firm, bring your left leg back to center and return to Mountain.

TEACHING NOTES ON BIG TOE HOLD

The practice above is my favorite modification for any beginner. Cueing students to lift the knee slightly higher than the hips and clasp the fingers just below the knee on the shin is accessible for most everyone. It's a great starting place to try different core cueing and to see what works with the group in front of you. Once they are stable in this beginning position, we can cue to take the bent knee out to the side to balance, resembling the action in the traditional version. Holding this position with the knee out to the side is more challenging, and again they can attempt to take their hand off of the knee. Balancing postures often create frustrations and negative internal chatter with new students, so I've given both of these modified options, the bent knee in front and the bent knee to the side, funny pose names to lighten the mood. I call bringing the knee up in front "Karate Kid," and sometimes I'll add bending and straightening the standing leg like Ralph Macchio did in the movie. If it is an appropriate group to make an alcohol reference, then I'll call the bent knee to the side position "Captain Morgan" from the rum commercial.

Although core awareness is particularly important when teaching standing one-legged balances, many other issues also arise in these balancing postures. In the case of Big Toe Hold, students struggle with even this modified version as they move their leg to the side trying to balance on one leg. I usually take students to the wall when I'm first teaching them this pose, to take the competition and stress out of learning to balance on one leg. The tension of trying to balance often causes students to lift up and grip in their shoulders and neck. In addition, they often shift their hip to the right when standing on the right leg (and vice versa) in an attempt to balance on their bones rather than engaging their muscles and using their core to stabilize.

Other issues with balance in this posture are similar to discussions we had in Chapter 4. For example, part of what creates stabilization in this pose is engaging the glutes, and many students, especially women, struggle with this in the one-legged balances. Sometimes, just reminding them to firm up the buttocks or asking them to imagine they are connecting their sit bones to their heels will help. Where the standing foot "points" was also discussed in reference to Warrior 3 in Chapter 4 and applies here also. Keeping the standing foot exactly straight forward does not work for all bodies.

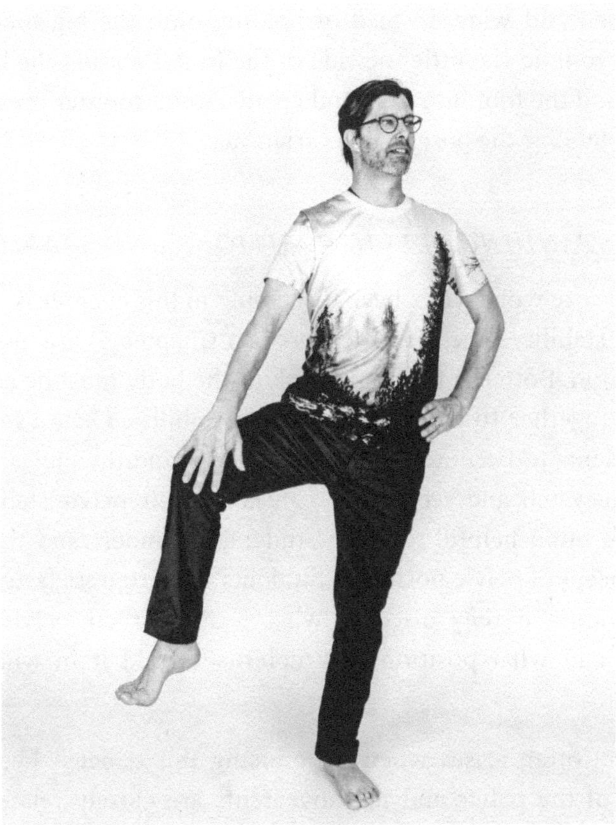

Many students have more success starting out with this modified version of Big Toe Hold with their knee bent.

Classically, the modification for this pose has been to put a strap around the elevated foot when it can't be reached with the hand. However, newer students often struggle with the strap and rock around while trying to balance, which is why I like to start with the bent knee modifications discussed above. For more experienced students, the strap works well after their hamstrings begin to loosen up. As these students begin working on the full pose, we need to watch their shoulders and upper backs while they reach for their feet. When I first tried to get into the full pose, I would round my shoulders over and sickle my ankle in an attempt to reach my toes. The shoulder blades need to be on the back and stable, with the collar bones open and wide. Instead of holding onto the big toe, another option is to hold the little toe side of the foot. Pressing the hand into the foot and the foot into the hand creates some counter pressure that helps to stabilize the pose in this variation.

UNDERSTANDING PELVIC POSITIONS AND STABILITY

All of the core work we've been discussing in this chapter is a big part of pelvic stability. The glutes (covered in Chapter 5) are also part of the equation. Both the front and back of the body must be active and working together to create strength and stability. Once I've encouraged students to become aware of their core and the glutes, the next step is to watch and see if they can keep their pelvis stable in the poses. It's often helpful to teach students to understand the underlying concept of pelvic positions. Students will progress faster in their understanding if they discover what position their pelvis likes to "rest" in and what position they habitually hold it in when doing asana.

Confusion often arises when introducing this concept because the position of the pelvis and its movements are closely related to the movements of the lumbar spine. When the top of our pelvis moves backwards our lumbar spine begins to flex, and when the top of our pelvis moves forward our low back begins to arch. In anatomy books, the movements of the pelvis and spine are separated, and different language is used to describe them.[4] The terms flexion and extension are used to describe the lumbar spine moving, but when we are focusing on just the movement of the pelvis, the term rotation is used. To feel the pelvis "rotating," focus on stabilizing your low back with your core. Place one hand on your belly and the other hand on your low back, and then see if you can experience your pelvis moving gently forward and backward without much movement in your spine. This subtle movement of the pelvis tilting forward and backwards is called rotation of the pelvis. I don't use the word rotation in classes, as it misleads some students into twisting their pelvis side to side. Anatomically, though, the word is a perfect description for how the pelvis rotates over the heads of the femur bones.

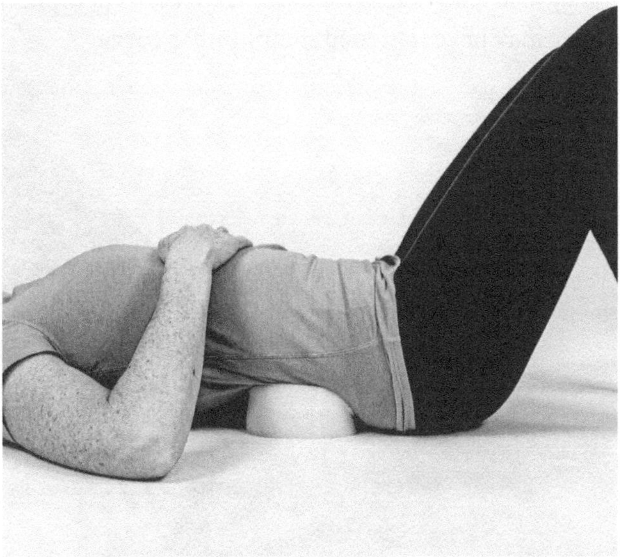

When the pelvis is in a neutral position the car wash sponge is slightly squished supporting a natural curve in the lumbar spine. The ribcage is also in a neutral position. The ASIS and the pubic bone appear to be in around the same plane.

I do try to teach students the language of pelvic positions, including anterior pelvic tilt, posterior pelvic tilt, and neutral pelvis. In Mountain, when the hip pointers move forward of the pubic bone and the low back begins to arch, this is called an anterior pelvic tilt. The opposite movement, when the hip pointers move back as the pubic bone moves forward and the low back begins to straighten, is called a posterior pelvic tilt. There are many factors that affect the position of the pelvis in individuals, including the tone and flexibility of the hamstrings, hip flexors, glutes, and core.

When students are first learning asana, we want them to learn to find these pelvic positions and to stabilize them. In many of the standing poses, we are teaching them to hold a neutral pelvis while also finding a natural healthy lumbar curve. In Tree, for example, a student with a habit of clenching their glutes together and tucking their tailbone under needs to be encouraged to release their glutes some. Their clenching habit creates a posterior pelvic tilt. Asking them to release the glutes may also lead to a more natural curve in their lumbar, as the tucking under may have flattened their lumbar curve.

The car wash sponge is squished as the student moves into a posterior pelvic tilt. The low back flattens out and the pelvis rotates towards the back. The public bone is slightly higher than the ASIS.

At the other extreme, if the student doesn't use their glutes or abdominals enough, thus sending their hip pointers forward into an anterior pelvic tilt, then we need to encourage them to engage the glutes and core to bring their pelvis to a neutral position. Again, this may also help to create a healthy lumbar curve rather than an overly arched back.

As the student lifts her ribcage up and arches her back she begins to move into an anterior pelvic tilt. The car wash sponge is less squished and the ASIS are slightly higher than the pubic bone.

A neutral position is somewhere in the middle between the two extremes and where it feels good to the student. Each person's "neutral" is unique. The bones of the pelvis can vary, and it can stress some students if we start talking in percentages and angles. If a student has a slight posterior or anterior tilt to their pelvis, but they have no pain or movement issues, then there is no need to focus in on it and create a problem where there isn't one. If they do yoga consistently, then over time they will likely improve their posture slowly and naturally. I use a big car wash sponge to help students learn to find their best neutral position, and to understand how to get into a posterior tilt and hold it when they need to.

Practice: Pelvic Tilts with a Big Car Wash Sponge

1. Lie on your back with your knees up and your feet on the mat.
2. Place your feet about hip-distance apart and a comfortable distance away from the buttocks.
3. Lift up your pelvis and place the car wash sponge horizontally under the top part of your sacrum and lowest lumbar vertebrae.
4. Bring your arms to the floor with your hands near your hips, and let your neck and jaw relax.
5. On an exhale press your pelvis to the floor and squish the sponge as much as you can. This is your posterior pelvic tilt.
6. Notice that your pubic bone is a little higher than your hip pointers. Also notice how your lumbar spine follows your posterior pelvic tilt and how as you continue with the movement, your lumbar spine begins to flatten onto the mat.
7. Inhale and begin to let your hip pointers rise up towards the ceiling while letting your pelvis rotate forward. Feel the sponge expand underneath you. This is your anterior pelvic tilt.
8. Notice how your pubic bone is now a little lower than your hip pointers. Your lumbar spine follows your anterior pelvic tilt, and as you continue with the movement, your lumbar spine begins to arch.
9. Keeping your lumbar spine as still as possible (it will move a little), gently rock your pelvis back and forth between these two positions, feeling your absolute range of motion in both directions.
10. Now, find some place in the middle of those two opposites. This is your neutral position. In your neutral position you will probably feel a little squish in your sponge, but it won't be flattened. Your pubic bone and your hip pointers will now be in the same plane (parallel with the floor in this case).

A Few Extra Cueing Ideas for Help with Anterior Tilts

Since yoga attracts people who are naturally flexible it is common to see students who "rest" in an anterior pelvic tilt. In many students one common situation is tight hip flexors and tight lower back muscles along with soft, unengaged glutes. Any imagery to help them feel heaviness at the bottom of the buttocks near the sit bones can help to release the lower back and encourage the glutes to engage. One example I like to use myself is to imagine there is sand in my back pockets. Another cue I like to use with a private session or students who already "get" imagery is to imagine that there are little hooks on the front (anterior side) of the sit bones. In Mountain, we imagine there is a dowel in front of the sit bones running parallel with the floor. We can "hook" the sit bones onto the dowel to hold the pelvis steady. If I say "hook your sit bones up" to these students, they will firm up their buttocks. This is a subtle action and when students are not experienced enough yet with imagery, they may just clamp the glutes together and tuck their tailbones under moving the pelvis too far into a posterior tilt (which as we talked about above, we don't want). You can try this imagery and then watch what the student does and then make corrections as needed.

FINDING THE CORE IN SIDE-LYING POSES AND EXERCISES

Side-lying poses and exercises are fantastic for challenging the core without over-taxing the joints of new students as they gain strength. As I went through a Pilates teacher training, I experienced how Joseph Pilates' side-lying leg lifts, circles, and kicks work well to get people into their abdominals. We can't lie on our side and move our top leg without using our core. As I began teaching a little mat Pilates in my classes, I watched as many yoga students, even supposedly advanced young yoga practitioners, fell over onto their backs when attempting a side-lying series. It became clear to me how many yoga students would just bypass using their core muscles and go to other patterns, like gripping in their low back, to stabilize themselves on their sides.

Since the majority of my students come to me for yoga, I began fusing the side-lying series from Pilates with something that looked more like yoga. The only side-lying pose described in B.K.S. Iyengar's famous book "Light on Yoga" is called Sleeping Vishnu[5]. I started fusing it with what I began to call Side-Lying Tree, and also Side-Lying Dancer. In between the yoga poses, I added a few Pilates leg lifts and circles to increase the challenge.

When I introduce these side poses to a group, I have the students put a big car wash sponge under their waists to remind them to lift and firm their side body. Some students complain that their hip hurts when they lie on their side, which is often the greater trochanter contacting the floor. In this case, I have them lie on their side with a blanket or a big sponge underneath the hip.

Practice: Side-Lying Flow with Sleeping Vishnu, Side-Lying Tree, and Side-Lying Dancer

1. Lie down on your mat on your right side and straighten your legs.
2. Place a big sponge under your right waist, keeping your waist lifted and your lowest floating ribs off of the mat.
3. Make sure that your feet, pelvis, and neck are all approximately along the same line (parallel to the long side of your mat) and elongate your spine. Place your left hand either in front of you for support or on your left hip.
4. Stretch your right arm along the line too and let your head rest on your arm. If it bothers your shoulder to stretch your arm over your head in this way, then bend your right elbow and let your head lie on the floor in your right palm. A block or blanket may also be used here if your neck needs more support.
5. Your right side is your foundation in this pose, so press the

little toe side of your right foot and your right palm into the mat and floor.

6. Draw your hip pointers towards each other and zip the belly together from pubic bone to belly button.
7. Relax your jaw and feel the breath moving your ribs.
8. Lift your left leg up just past hip height, externally rotate your left hip, and then lift it up as high as you can without anything hurting. Flex your left foot.
9. If your hamstrings are less flexible, then bend your left leg and bring your left hand behind your left thigh to support your leg.
10. Keep pressing into the mat with the little toe side of your right foot and your right hand to help maintain your stability.
11. If your hamstrings allow, you may choose to extend your left leg out long, lifting it up towards the ceiling, and pressing your left hand into the little toe side of your left foot.
12. Breathe and balance in the pose while continuing to feel yourself getting longer on the mat.
13. When you come out of the pose, imagine that your left leg is getting longer. As you take your entire exhale to lower the leg, fully extend it and lay it on top of the bottom leg.
14. While keeping this same foundation of pressing the little toe side of the right foot and the right palm into the mat, move your left foot into Tree position, pressing your left foot gently into your right inner thigh.
15. Your left fingertips can be placed on the floor in front of you to help balance.
16. Elongate your spine as you imagine that you are lengthening your ribs away from your hips, and then see if you can stretch your left arm over your head, coming into the Tree on your side.
17. Once you are stable, try turning your right palm up so that your palms can face each other.
18. Relax the jaw and let the muscles of the neck get quiet. Feel your core holding you steady on your side.

19. For an extra challenge, try to slowly transition to Side-Lying Dancer without rocking around or rolling over. Turn your right palm back down and press it into the floor to stabilize. Then move the left foot behind you and reach back with your left hand to grasp the little toe side of your foot.
20. Press your hand into your foot and your foot into your hand. Keep your belly zipped up as you stretch into a gentle backbend.
21. To come out of the pose, take an inhale to prepare and then on an exhale continue to press into the mat with your right side as you release your left foot. Stretch the left leg long and bring it down to rest on your right leg.

Side-Lying Tree with the arm under the head for support is a great option for beginners to build core strength.

MY THOUGHTS ON TRADITIONAL ABDOMINAL EXERCISES AND LUMBAR FLEXION

Lumbar flexion is often avoided by yoga teachers due to a number of factors. First, we have all been taught that it is safer for students to elongate their spines in forward bends. Second, yoga culture has emphasized the big backbending poses in the media and in trainings. Finally, because the majority of the most commonly taught yoga poses don't call for spinal flexion, the focus is usually on elongation, twisting, or backbending. This lack of focus on flexion, especially lumbar flexion (along with a posterior pelvic tilt), becomes apparent when students try to learn poses that require it, such as Half Boat, Crow, and Tortoise. I've seen videos of yogis doing Crow with a flat lumbar spine and excessive rounding in the thoracic. In many of these cases, they are using more of their back and shoulder muscles to stabilize the pose than their abdominals. All of this has been exacerbated by the idea in some yoga circles that any abdominal flexion exercise will "flatten" or hurt students' backs.

I think the body only gets out of balance when the same set of exercises is done over and over, day after day. Since most clients will not do repetitive exercises daily, we don't really need to worry about students "flattening" their backs. That said, I have seen Pilates instructors create pain and dysfunction in their pelvic floor from only focusing on the posterior pelvic tilt and their TA all the time. In addition, some of the classic curling sit-ups that work the RA are often hard on the low back, and if they are overdone, they can even create disc problems. At the other extreme, I've watched an entire group of women who were into a predominately backbending style of yoga develop a walking gait that included a sway back with their ribs popped forward. This developed over a few years from practicing progressively bigger and bigger backbending with every session. The key here, of course, is balance. If we want to help students learn to fly their Crow or hold Half Boat, then we need to get them interested in both sides of their body.

Before adding classic abdominals to our classes, we need to review what is going on with our students' pelvises and low backs. Most people sit too much all day with their low back in flexion, creating tightness and soreness. This means that most students coming into classes today need to do some gentle backbending. What these students don't need is a lot of abdominal curls. As more yoga is taught in gyms, there is increasing pressure to include "abs" in the class. Many students have the idea that they have to do crunches to get stronger or develop the desired flat stomach look, but as we've discussed throughout this chapter, we can learn to work the core in many poses. An easy way to distract a gym class from abdominals is to transition the group into holding forearm planks. Forearm planks, especially when we add the bone cues in this chapter to the challenge, are a safer way to build core strength in a mixed group than classic curls. However, for those students who have a healthy posture and who are working on progressing deeper into more advanced yoga poses, some well-taught classic Pilates flexion exercises may be appropriate and helpful.

Awaken + Stabilize + Strengthen

An effective way to teach students to stabilize and strengthen their core includes creative cueing in one-legged postures, variations of Opposite Arm Leg balance (Bird Dog), and side-lying flows. The old school classic curls and cues to pull the belly button to the spine are not as effective for creating core strength and can put students at risk for injury. By guiding students into a better understanding of pelvic positions and the core, we will help them improve not only the asana but their daily movement and quality of life.

7

FREEING THE SPINE

As teachers we want our own spines, and those of our students, to be able to move freely with a quality of smoothness, suppleness, and strength. A healthy spine moves easily and painlessly throughout our daily activities. For those who must sit much of their day at work, the entire spine becomes less mobile and gets stuck to some degree in a flexed (rounded) position. When the body becomes accustomed to this slumped position all day, it keeps returning to that position even when not at work. Our job as yoga teachers is to guide our students into awareness of their posture and the condition of their own backs. Once students understand their own postural issues, they can begin making alignment changes in their yoga postures and in their daily activities. In this chapter we will focus on safely cueing the spine into forward bends, backbends, and twists that will help our students restore the natural curves and range of motion of their spines.

BASIC SPINAL ANATOMY REVIEW

Not every yoga teacher needs or wants to go deeply into anatomy studies, but all teachers should have a basic understanding of how the spine works and where and how injuries can occur in yoga class. Injuries occur most often in the lumbar and the cervical spine because these areas have the largest amount of movement. The thoracic spine is rarely injured in yoga or in any group exercise class due to its stability with the attached ribs. Our hearts are contained and protected by the strong thoracic vertebrae, so mechanical injuries generally only occur in this area with accidents.

Before we dive into the asana, let's do a quick review of basic spinal anatomy and movement. We have 24 vertebrae with intervertebral discs in between that are grouped into 3 areas of the spine called the cervical, the thoracic, and the lumbar regions. Each area of the spine moves differently depending on the variations of vertebrae shapes, the size of the intervertebral discs, and where the ribs attach. We describe the movements of the spine as flexion (forward folding), extension (backbending), lateral flexion (side bending), and rotation (twisting).

Our cervical spine starts at the base of the skull and ends at the base of the neck. This includes 7 vertebrae labeled C1 through C7. C1 is at the top of the spine and along with C2 it allows a wide range of motion for our skull. All the cervical vertebrae allow for a high range of extension, flexion, and rotation of our necks so we can look in all directions as we go about our daily tasks. Although we can flex our necks to the side, the cervical vertebrae do not allow a deep sideways movement. The intervertebral discs in the cervical section of our spine are a little thicker than those in the thoracic to allow for all the movement needed. The thoracic spine starts at the base of the neck with T1 and ends near the bottom of the rib cage at T12. These 12 vertebrae and their discs allow for less movement in general than other areas of the spine in part because the ribs are attached.

The middle of the thoracic spine behind the heart has the least amount of movement as it functions along with the sternum (on the chest) to create stability and protect our hearts. Despite the greater rigidity, the thoracic spine still allows for some extension, flexion, side flexion, and rotation. The area that allows for the most rotation is the T11 and T12 at the base of the rib cage where we find the floating ribs.

Average ROM (in Degrees) of Different Spinal Areas[1]

	CERVICAL	THORACIC	LUMBAR
FLEXION	65	35	50
EXTENSION	40	25	35
LATERAL FLEXION	35	20	20
ROTATION	50	35	5

The lumbar spine starts near the base of the rib cage with L1 and ends at the bottom of the spine just above the sacrum at L5. These 5 vertebrae and their discs allow for a high range of extension and flexion. This is where much of the back bending and forward bending occurs in our spines. The lumbar spine also allows for side flexion, but it is very limited in terms of rotation. The intervertebral discs in the lumbar are thicker than in the thoracic to allow for the larger range of motion.

When we teach yoga, we encourage our students to lengthen the spine, creating a healthy posture. Cues such as "reach the crown of your head upward," or "imagine there is a string at the top of your head pulling you upward," are meant to elongate the spine. All areas of the spine can elongate gently. At night when we sleep, our discs rehydrate and "plump up," making many of us slightly taller first thing in the morning.[2] When we learn to elongate and improve our posture in daily living, this helps keep our spines supple and free.

WHY THE LUMBAR IS AT RISK IN FORWARD BENDS

After seeing photos of incredibly deep backbends in yoga ads and on social media, one might think that students are most often injured doing big backbends. When it comes to beginning students, however, the possibility of injury is probably greater in forward bending. Whether they have tight hips and/or hamstrings, or simply move first with the muscles of the lumbar spine, their pelvis often doesn't move much when they try to forward bend. All the movement happens in the lumbar area. Once they get as far over as they can go, they hang, trying to reach their toes. With their backs rounded they are loading their lumbar with weight and putting pressure on the disc walls. This is called *loaded flexion,* and it can cause injuries over time. When the spine flexes, the nucleus (inner core) of each disc moves backwards, putting pressure on the disc's wall. Over time, this can contribute to herniated discs and other issues.

In addition, as people age and continue to sit much of the day, the muscles in their backs become weak and tight. Discs naturally begin to dry out over time. In some cases, as the discs are affected by poor posture and aging, they move and bulge. This puts pressure on nerve roots, causing numbness and pain in the hips and legs. Knowing all this, as teachers we need to sequence and cue our beginning and mixed classes to reduce the amount of forward bending, especially in the beginning of class before the hips and legs are warm, and also to encourage modifications and a relaxed attitude. Students who pull intensely on yoga straps with the hands, bounce up and down trying to touch the toes, or hang unengaged in standing forward bends, may develop issues in the lumbar spine over time.

Elongating the Spine in Seated Forward Folds

Students can hear a teacher cueing them to sit up straight, understand that request, and still not be able to do it. Many new students will think that they are sitting up straight but are actually rounded over a little. When we cue students to "straighten their spine," we are asking them to elongate the spine while keeping the natural, healthy curves.

To help students understand the movement fundamental of elongating their spines, introducing a long dowel[3] as a teaching tool works well. Place a dowel along the spine of the students while they are sitting in Staff and ask them to feel the dowel on the back of their pelvis, in the middle of their thoracic, and at the back of their head. Ask them to elongate along the dowel while feeling the natural curves in their spines. There should be some natural space between the dowel and the lumbar region, and also some space between the dowel and the cervical spine.

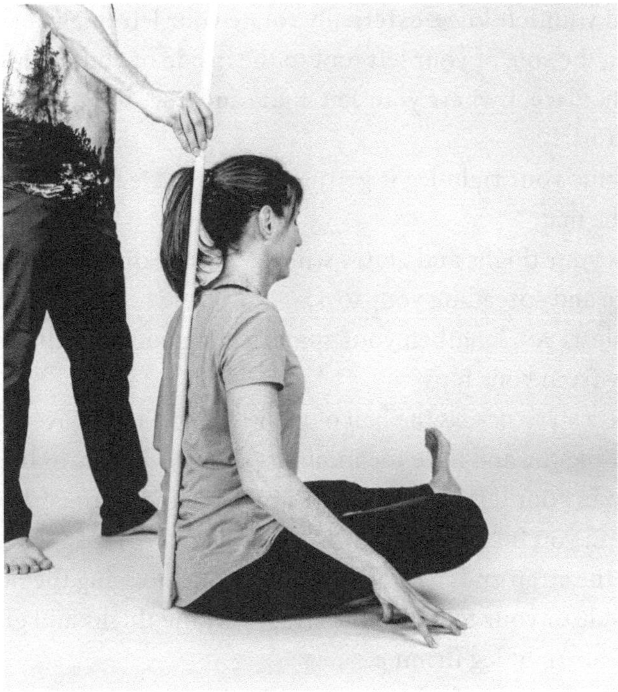

Holding a dowel along the student's spine helps provide feedback to them about their posture and position.

Once students can connect with the feeling of a long spine in Staff, then they can begin to fold forward at the hips while keeping their spines stable. In seated forward folds, new students often round over, and we have to keep reminding them to lengthen out and fold at their hips. Let's try lengthening the spine and folding at the hips in Head to Knee.

Practice: Basic Head to Knee

1. Sit with your legs long in front of you and your feet about hip-distance apart.
2. Sit up as tall as you can, using your hands or fingertips behind you for support.
3. Zip your belly up from your pubic bone to your belly button, and feel both of your sit bones ground down into the mat.
4. Bend your left knee, externally rotate your left thigh, and bring the sole of your left foot to the inside of your right thigh. Place it where your left ankle and knee are the most comfortable.
5. Imagine your right leg is getting longer and feel it get heavy on the mat.
6. Firm your thighs and glutes while gently flexing your right ankle and spreading your toes.
7. Inhale as you lengthen your spine, feeling your ribs lift up away from your hips.
8. Place a strap across the ball of your foot so that it covers your right big toe and little toe mounds. Hold both ends of the strap in your left hand. Place your right hand or fingertips behind you for support.
9. Pull the strap ends gently to the left while pressing the little toe side of your foot into the strap. Feel the thighs and glutes on your right leg firming.
10. If you are able to fold forward with a long spine, then begin to fold over your legs. Feel the top of your pelvis moving forward and downward towards your thigh bones.
11. Remember to keep your back long rather than rounding over.

If you can't fold forward without rounding, then work on sitting up straight instead.

12. Bring your right fingertips to the side of your right leg, press the fingers into the floor and draw them back isometrically to help support the lengthening of your spine.
13. Continue to breathe into the ribs, feeling them moving as the pose continues to develop.
14. Feel your shoulder blades on your back as you keep your collar bones open and wide and your upper back elongated.
15. Keeping your neck in line with your spine, reach the crown of your head away from your hips. As you elongate the back of your neck, see if you can feel the muscles of your throat begin to tone.
16. To come out of the pose, release the strap and place your hands behind you for support as you return to a relaxed seated position.

MODIFICATIONS AND CUES FOR THE LESS FLEXIBLE STUDENTS IN SEATED FORWARD FOLD

For those of us who have always been flexible, "going to the floor" towards the end of a yoga class is something we look forward to. It comes easily to us, and we enjoy it. Since flexible people are often attracted to yoga and to teaching, we must remember how uncomfortable seated forward folds are for less flexible students. Just sitting on the floor can be painful and uncomfortable, and these students often make little progress over time without proper modifications and cueing. For some people, just sitting in Staff is difficult, as their hip flexors burn at the hip creases and their backs ache or spasm. As stated above, one of the important concepts to impart to new students is that we are trying to move from the hips in forward bends, not by rounding the back over and dropping the head. When students are tight in the hips and low backs, there is often not a lot of movement to be had at first in forward bends, and they get frustrated.

Offering props to these students so they can sit up straighter often reduces their discomfort. Ask them to sit on blocks or blankets with their hands behind them to help keep their spines long. Getting them up higher reduces the angle of flexion in the hips and sometimes quiets the hip flexors. Sitting up against a wall, which supports the back, is also effective for those who are struggling. For students with less flexibility in the hamstrings, putting blocks, rolled blankets, or even some big car wash sponges under their knees relieves the pain of the hamstring tendons pulling at the back of the knees. When the knees are bent, students often can get a little more movement in the hips.

Another teaching tool is to place a sandbag on the ankle of the straight leg in Head to Knee, and in other seated forward folds where one or both legs are straight. The weight of the sandbag helps to quiet the hip flexors, and the student will often connect better with their core. It reduces the discomfort just enough for people to feel their legs getting heavy and longer as they engage their muscles. Although it should not be used all the time, it is a great tool to help students feel the comfort they are trying to find on their own. If they react positively to the sandbag, then have them take the bag off and try the pose again without it. Can they feel their legs getting heavy, grounded, and long? Encourage them to find that same balance of work and comfort in their seated forward folds without the sandbag.

For students who are much less flexible, and for those who have a history of herniated discs or other back problems, it is safer to have them stretch their hamstrings and hips lying on their backs. This keeps the lumbar spine stable, because they can only flex it enough to imprint their low back onto the mat, which is nowhere near the degree of flexion they can do while sitting. We want to encourage them to try to keep a natural little curve in their low back, but for this type of student it is very difficult. In order to help them feel a gentle curve in the lumbar spine, I'll have them place a big car wash sponge under their low back and partially contacting the back of the pelvis near the top of the sacrum. Although they will probably completely squish the sponge a first, it will at least help them become aware of the position of their pelvis and the flexion in their backs.

WORKING STUDENTS INTO BEGINNING BACKBENDS

As we've been discussing the issues with forward bending and our students spending much of their day slumped over desks, the solution has become obvious: they need backbends! It is crucial to add gentle backbends to almost any beginning or mixed level class. Since most people don't get enough extension in their daily lives, they are sometimes resistant to the backbending section of class. For some students, backbending doesn't feel natural to them and isn't that comfortable at first. Since we are addicted to flexion, it can take someone who is truly out of shape awhile to appreciate how great a little Locust or Cobra can make them feel. One of my students would grunt and groan whenever we did backbends, and he came up with what he called a new tagline for my studio, "What fresh hell is this?" Needless to say, I did not use his idea to market my studio, but his sense of humor helped me to understand just how much of a struggle backbending is for new students.

When introducing backbending, the best practice is to start with gentle Cobra or Locust poses. Watch your students move and see where the backbend is happening along their spines. It is common for beginners to focus the backbend in their lumbar area and have little extension in the thoracic area. There may even be one area of the lumbar curve where most of the extension is happening. What we would like to see is some extension all along the spine, even in the upper thoracic region. In Cobra, if we cue to lift the heart first, keep the muscles of the throat toned, and then lift the head up last, it encourages students to work more in their thoracic spines. For more information about working the front of the throat in backbending, see Chapter 10.

For many years in both yoga and fitness classes, a common cue has been to "press the pubic bone into the mat" when teaching backbends like Locust and Cobra. I think the original idea behind this cue was to stabilize the pelvis and get the lower abdominals working. Although we do want to tone our low belly, pressing the pubic bone into the mat often introduces other problems, as students frequently over-squeeze the large buttocks muscle, gluteus maximus, with this cue. We do want students to tone their glutes in backbends, but when they overuse their gluteus maximus muscles and squeeze the buttocks together, it causes the top of the pelvis to move backwards into a posterior pelvic tilt. This can lock up the low back and sacral area while also hardening the hip flexors on the front body near the hip creases. We need the front body to open up and stretch in order to come into a nice even backbend. Start with some kind of a core cue from Chapter 6, like "zipping the belly together from pubic bone to belly button," and then ask the students to feel the pubic bone either resting on the mat or slightly lifted off the mat. This will take the pinch out of the lumbar area for many students.

Get off your mat, walk around the room, and observe your students as they work through a basic Locust series; watch to see how many of them are squeezing their buttocks together when they lift up their legs. If you have enough of them doing this, then get them up and try working through the cues we discussed in Chapter 4 for learning to tone the glutes without squeezing them together. Some students will have to learn to relax the large gluteal muscles first, and then add them back in with a gentler toning. It's better to teach awareness of this fundamental first before moving into bigger backbends. If students attempt to push up into a full backbend while squeezing the glutes together and shoving their pubic bone to the sky, they may create compression in their low back and SI joints. Over time, this lack of awareness may create injuries.

Practice: Locust

1. Lie on your belly and stack your hands under your forehead.
2. Lengthen your body on the mat, reaching the crown of your head in one direction and your toes in the other.

3. Imagine you have a drawstring wrapped around your pelvis. Feel it firm around you and tie it in the back near the top of your sacrum.
4. Point your toes and press the tops of your feet into the mat while also firming your thighs.
5. Feel your hip pointers drawing towards each other as you zip your belly up from pubic bone to belly button.
6. Also see if you can engage your upper abdominals. Try imagining that your lowest ribs are drawing in and up a little. If that doesn't work for you, then try imagining your lowest ribs are reaching down energetically towards your hip pointers.
7. Keeping this core awareness, stretch your arms out on the floor comfortably by your sides with your palms facing up.
8. Keeping your head bowed at first, lift your chest off the mat a little. Tone the muscles at the front of your throat, and then lead with your chest as you lift up a little more, letting your head and gaze be the last thing to come up. Once in the pose, avoid throwing your head back. Instead, keep your head in a neutral position and your neck in line with your spine.
9. As you lift up your arms, feel your shoulder blades move towards each other on your back as your collar bone area widens.
10. Keeping your chest, head, and arms elevated, lift your legs up off the mat. If you feel your buttocks squeezing together, then lower your legs down and work to get some tone in the glutes without gripping them inward and try again.
11. Imagine your legs feel like they are getting longer, and engage as if you are trying to move them away from each other but you can't.
12. When you lower down from the pose, stack your hands again under your forehead, and then turn your head to the side and rest. Breathe into your low back. On the exhale, release and let the pelvis feel heavy on the mat.

Opening the Front Body First for Backbends

Getting into bigger and bigger backbends and finally into full Wheel is a common goal with new students. Our job is to guide them into improving their posture first and then have them learn to extend throughout the whole spine. At first, new students often backbend only in their lumbar spines, even if they don't intend to. This becomes especially true in poses like Camel and Bow, where they want to reach their feet. The focus initially is often on the back body, trying to gain flexibility in the lumbar area. However, what frequently keeps students from progressing into a full backbend is actually tightness in their front body. Tight quadriceps and pectorals often put the brakes on backbending.

Traditionally, Hero has been recommended as not only a quadricep stretch but a whole front body stretch in preparation for full back-bend. For those whose knees can tolerate the pose, it definitely works, but many won't feel comfortable in the pose even when sitting on a block. There are safer ways to stretch the quadriceps in beginning and mixed level classes, such as a gentle Dancer pose at the wall, starting with a standing quadricep stretch and then lifting up into a small backbend. Quadricep stretches in low lunge with the back knee down are also more accessible to many beginning students than Hero.

Tight pectorals not only contribute to the common problem of the shoulders being rolled forward, but they also keep students from extending into their thoracic spine. In addition, these students also have a forward head posture, and they must first work on improving their posture with basic standing poses and gentle backbends before trying to progress to a full backbend. It is helpful to start with a series of standing poses with various arm positions to warm up the shoulders. After some basic Warrior 1 and 2 poses, we can add in arm variations into standing poses that include the hands clasped behind the back and cueing to open the chest while bringing the shoulder blades onto the back. For those with less flexible shoulders, we can modify this by having students place their hands, palms out, on the back of their pelvis. For more about shoulder flexibility and awareness, see our discussion in Chapter 9.

LEARNING TO TWIST THROUGH THE RIBS

When new students start to learn twisting, a number of issues often arise. First, people tend to just move their shoulder blades around their back, making it look like they are twisting to the untrained eye, but with very little twist actually occurring in their spine. Second, if the twist doesn't come easily, they tend to just move their hips in space rather than rotate the spine as much. Finally, many students, in an attempt to get further into the twists, use their shoulders to crank their torsos around. Although it is certainly fine to let the hands and shoulders help, they should not be driving the twist. We want to guide students to initiate twisting with their abdominals.

A true spinal twist happens mostly in the thoracic spine, especially around T11 and T12. Our lumbar vertebrae are not meant to twist; most anatomy charts list the lumbar rotational ability at less than 5% (see the chart at the beginning of this chapter). When students do not stabilize their pelvis and lumbar spine when trying to twist, they can create low back pain and aggravate injuries. When we initiate the movement of a twist within our abdominals, we will first feel the movement in our ribs and side waists. As we get better at this abdominal engagement, the body begins to heat up from within, and yogis will begin to sweat doing twists, even reclined ones!

Practice: Teaching Abdominal Awareness in Twisting

1. Sit in Easy pose on your mat. If it helps you be more comfortable, then sit on a blanket or a block.
2. Place your fingertips on the floor on each side of you for support. Zip up your belly from pubic bone to belly button, toning your low belly.
3. Feel the back of your pelvis get heavy and release downward, grounding your sit bones.

4. Lengthen your spine, feeling your rib cage rise up from your grounded pelvis.
5. Place your hands on your shoulders. Let your elbows be out to each side, making sure you haven't lifted your shoulders up towards your ears, creating tension in your neck.
6. Firm your shoulder blades onto your back and keep them in place as you begin to twist your ribs towards the right.
7. Feel the low left side of your belly toning as you continue twisting to the right. Allow your left hip to follow the twist a little as your ribs rotate even more.
8. Keep your elbows and your shoulder blades quiet, and feel the muscles in your belly and sides moving your ribs.
9. Resist the urge to put your hands on your right thigh and pull yourself deeper into the twist. Experience how far you can get into the twist without using your hands to move your shoulders.
10. Let your neck and head be the last to twist, and avoid leading with your eyes. Twist your neck only as much as is comfortable.
11. When you come to the end of your rotation, let your hands come down and place your left hand on your right thigh and your right fingertips on the floor in a comfortable position.
12. While your shoulder blades remain firmly in place, let your hands and shoulders gently deepen the twist. Using your shoulders for twisting should be like the icing on the cake. It's the little extra that makes it better.
13. To come out of the twist, keep your core engaged as you return to Easy pose.

TEACHING NOTES ON REVOLVED STANDING POSES

Whether we are teaching Revolved Triangle, Revolved Half Moon, or a twisted lunge variation, many of the same issues arise in the pelvis, the neck, and the shoulders. Traditionally in all three of these poses, the cue has been to level the pelvis parallel to the floor. Although many yogis still enjoy this traditional alignment, it is not accessible or safe for everyone. When we twist, it is natural for our hips to follow our torso. If you are not sure what I mean, then put your hands on your hips, twist to the right, and feel your left hip moving a little with you. When I twist to the right, I feel my left hip follow the twist a little at first, and then it stabilizes as I tone my low belly towards the left, and the twist moves into my thoracic spine. My pelvis isn't perfectly level, but close. I've moved away from cueing the pelvis in these postures and instead focus on cueing the core and twisting through the ribs. The hips end up naturally where they need to be. Students with SI joint issues will do better letting their hips follow the twist, and they may not look level at all; forcing the pelvis to be level with these students may aggravate their issues. The takeaway here is that some people can do the traditional alignment safely, and others cannot. Forcing everyone into the same form doesn't allow for our physical differences. Our focus should be on how students feel in the poses, and not how they look.

Another common issue is for beginners to lead with their head and eyes into twists. When the eyes lead, this tends to cause the muscles on the back of the neck, especially those at the base of the skull, to grip and pinch. After twisting the neck first, students get stuck or locked up in the neck region, often experience discomfort, and find that the rotational mobility of their spine doesn't improve. Before starting the twist, we can cue students to keep their gaze focused on the tip of their noses or straight forward while they initiate the twist from their side waists. Moving from the abdominals, then the heart, and then finally the head and eyes will take the pinch out of these poses. For more on this topic, see Chapter 10.

Lastly, in an attempt to look like the photographs of flexible people in these rotated poses, students try to reach their top hand straight up. They pinch the back of their shoulder when their ribs do not rotate around enough. This is usually accompanied by too much extension in the neck as they try to look up. The solution is to have them just keep their top hand on their hip and start by focusing on rotating the ribs.

Make Revolved Triangle more accessible by offering the option of placing a block under the hand, and letting the pelvis follow the twist a little.

Practice: Modified Revolved Triangle

1. From Mountain, place two blocks in front of you on your mat, one on each side of your feet. Then, take a comfortable step back with your right foot.
2. Turn your back hip out just a little with your right foot at a comfortable angle.
3. Place your heels in a line or a little wider.
4. Engage your core by plugging it in and lifting it up.
5. With your hands on your hips, lengthen your spine while reaching the crown of your head towards the ceiling.
6. Feel your breath moving your ribs.

7. Ground into your heels and big toe mounds. Feel the energy coming in and up through your arches.
8. Firm your quads and your glutes as you forward fold into Pyramid.
9. Place your hands on the blocks on either side of your front leg and lengthen your spine parallel to the floor. If you have trouble getting your hands to the blocks and feel your back rounding, then get a chair and put your hands on the chair seat.
10. Keeping the legs firm and the feet rooted, shift your pelvis a little to the right to ground your outer right heel.
11. Now shift your ribs gently to the left over your front leg.
12. Take a moment here to firm and lengthen again.
13. Move a block to the inside of your front ankle, and ground your right fingertips on the block.
14. Place your left hand on your left hip.
15. Firm your low belly towards the right and begin twisting your ribs to the left. Let your right hip follow the twist a little if that feels best for you.
16. As you are twisting, let your gaze be on the floor at first. Let your abdominals initiate the movement, then feel the ribs move, then the chest. Finally, the head turns to the left.
17. Leave your left hand on your hip until you have twisted as far as you can comfortably.
18. When you've twisted as far as you can go, then stretch your left arm up and see if it is comfortable for you. If your shoulder or neck feels pinched or painful in any way, then place the hand back on the left hip and just work on twisting the ribs.
19. Let the palm of the right hand come onto the block and grasp the block with your thumb on the inside.
20. Keeping your shoulder blades firmly on your back, press your thumb gently into the grounded block to help deepen the twist.
21. Feel the breath coming in and out, moving the ribs.

22. To come out of the pose, keep your core and legs firm as you untwist. Then, while softening the knees, bring your hands to your hips, keeping your back long as you return to Mountain.

Sequencing for Standing Revolved Poses

For many beginners, the standing revolved poses can initially be very challenging. We can still teach these poses to most beginners with modifications and the proper warm-up. For mixed level classes that include beginners, these poses need to be sequenced towards the end of the standing sequences and after warming up the hips, knees, hamstrings, core, and shoulders. A good place to start is with basic sequences including Warrior 1, Warrior 2, Side Angle, and Triangle. If the group can handle some shoulder and wrist work, then add in some simple Sun Salutations to warm up the whole body. For those who can't tolerate Sun Salutations, for whatever reason, additional standing sequences will also warm and prepare the body for the standing twisted postures. A tight side body makes twisting more difficult, so it works well to add in warm-ups like standing side stretches in Mountain, basic twisted lunges, and Dancing Warrior (sometimes called Reverse Warrior) to the standing sequences. In Revolved Half Moon and Revolved Triangle, students often complain about the outer hip and the IT Band of the standing leg. Working with some Standing Wide-Legged Forward Bend variations, including walking the hands from one side to the other and the classic twisted version, are great preparations.

USING THE BREATH TO DEEPEN THE TWISTING EXPERIENCE

Once students have been around for a while, I like to start adding more subtle work and see if they take to it. We can learn to deepen twists by breathing more into one lung than the other. The breath will help to rotate the rib cage a little, deepening the experience. The first hurdle is to convince students that they can indeed breathe more into one lung more than the other. We are designed this way so that if there is a problem with one lung, then we can rely on the other. Many people are not really aware of their ability to do this, and sometimes it takes a while for students to be able to connect with it. For me, this subtle work is where we can advance our practice. Once you connect with this breathing rotation, you can add it into any twist for a deeper experience.

Practice: Rotating the Rib Cage Subtly with the Breath

1. Sit in a comfortable position and place your hands on each side of your body on your ribs.
2. Focus on your right lung and feel the breath coming in.
3. On each inhale, try to focus on breathing more into your right lung and see if you can feel your ribs move on your right side.
4. Work on the right side for a few more breaths, feeling the right ribs moving more than the left ones.
5. Then switch and focus on inhaling into your left lung and feeling the left ribs move.
6. Once you've gotten the hang of breathing more into one side, you can try feeling a subtle rotation occurring.
7. Keeping your hands on your ribs imagine you are inhaling into your lowest left back ribs.
8. Let the breath feel like it is filling in that area and then expanding. You may feel your rib cage start to twist to the right.
9. Try it on the other side also and see what you find.

INTRODUCING PINWHEEL

In my own exploration of movement, I found a seated twist that I liked doing. It felt similar to moves I had learned taking modern dance classes in college. At some point early in my yoga life, I remember that I saw another older teacher show it to me, but it is not listed in any of the newer books. After consulting with some yoga teacher friends around the country, we decided that it has indeed been taught in a few yoga circles over the years under various names.[4] My favorite name that I felt was the most appropriate for the pose is Pinwheel. When I include twists in the pose, we call it Revolved Pinwheel at our studio. Pinwheel looks somewhat like Pigeon, but we shift our weight over onto one hip and bend both knees.

Pinwheel is an option for students who struggle with Pigeon.

Some teachers use the basic Pinwheel as a modification for Pigeon for those students who have tight hips or knee problems. This certainly is an option that works. Pinwheel gives the less flexible students with knee issues another option other than doing Pigeon on their back. In my studio the Revolved Pinwheel has been around for many years as a big reclined twist that I sequence in towards the end of the class. I like to teach it in a sitting flow with a modified Rishi twist, including side stretches that are reminiscent of the Pilates Mermaid exercise. Once in the pose, we can try rotating a little deeper with our breath.

Practice: Revolved Pinwheel with Alternative Side Breathing

1. From Staff, bend your knees and bring your feet to your left side so that you are sitting on your right hip.
2. Keep the knees bent between 45 and 90 degrees, and separate the legs just enough to create a little space between the right foot and the left knee.
3. Bring your hands to the floor to the right side of your right thigh.
4. Firm your thighs and flex your feet.
5. Draw your hip pointers towards each other, activating your core.
6. Imagine that below your belly button your belly is moving towards the left, and then begin to twist your ribs toward your right, walking your hands around into a comfortable twist.
7. Allow your left hip to follow the ribs a little as you twist to the right. Bring your elbows onto the mat under your shoulders and rest on your forearms.
8. Bring your breath in your back low left ribs and feel yourself subtly twisting to the right.
9. If comfortable, come further into the pose by resting your head on your hands or fists and let the jaw and the neck relax.
10. Breathe into your low left ribs again, feeling the breath moving the body.
11. To come out, keep your core and thighs toned as you use your hands to press up to sitting, unwind, and return to Staff.

Elongation + Core Engagement + Breath

As we guide students to stronger, healthier spines, we can reduce injuries and increase success by offering modifications and options. Reducing the number of forward bends in our mixed level classes is helpful, along with cueing an elongated, supported spine when we do forward fold. We can instead offer less flexible students the option of stretching their hips and hamstrings while lying on their back.

Keeping the core engaged, whether in forward bends, backbends, or twists, helps to support and protect our spines as we practice. Rather than relying on continually deeper ROM as a goal, we can focus on the sensations of our breath in the postures, taking us deeper into the body and our practice.

8
STABILIZING THE SHOULDERS AND OPENING THE CHEST

As we have been discussing in previous chapters, students often come to class with an unhealthy posture, including shoulders that are rolled forward, tight pectoral muscles, head forward of the shoulders, and a rounded upper back. In addition to sitting in "deskasana" all day, many also arrive at yoga class with shoulders that are already irritated or injured in some way. Small rotator cuff injuries are commonly acquired through daily activities like housework, yard work, and weekend athletic pursuits. These small injuries and tears heal on their own, only to be injured or inflamed again with intense overuse such as gardening all weekend or playing tennis all day.

Some of the most popular yoga flow classes include many Sun Salutations, Downward Dogs, and Side Planks. All of these require the entire shoulder to be well stabilized, properly aligned, and strong. When students with postural issues and/or underlying shoulder irritation attempt too many of these postures before addressing the problems, they are at risk of injury. First, we need to guide students into awareness of their shoulders and posture, and then we can move towards opening their chests and also strengthening their upper backs and shoulders.

TEACHING STUDENTS HOW THEIR SHOULDERS WORK

Understanding how the shoulders work and move is an important first lesson for all new yoga students. They also need to understand where their shoulders should align in healthy posture. There are a few quick teaching tools we can run through when new students arrive to encourage understanding.

Practice: Protraction/Retraction and Elevation/Depression of the Shoulder Blades

1. Stand in Mountain with your arms relaxed at your sides.
2. Ground your feet into the mat, firm your thighs and elongate your spine.
3. Widen through your collarbones and relax your jaw.
4. Place your hands out in front of you to shoulder height with the palms facing each other.
5. While keeping your arms extended, reach your hands away from your body as if you are handing someone something. Do not bend your elbows.
6. Feel your shoulder blades move away from each other and the spine, while your upper back rounds. This is called protraction.
7. Keeping your arms long and without bending your elbows, draw your arm bones straight back.
8. Feel your shoulder blades coming towards each other and moving closer to your spine. This is called retraction.
9. Go back and forth between the two positions a few times and notice your range of motion at both extremes of shoulder blade protraction and retraction.
10. Next, bring your shoulder blades into a neutral position with

your blades somewhere in the middle of the two end ranges that you just experienced.

11. Keep the palms of the hands facing each other and take your hands over your head.
12. Now lift your shoulders as far up towards your ears as you can. This is called elevation.
13. While keeping your hands overhead with your palms facing each other, draw your shoulder blades as far down your back as you can. This is called depression.
14. Move back and forth from your highest shoulder blade elevation to your lowest shoulder blade depression and experience your own range of movement (ROM).
15. Now find a neutral position with your blades somewhere in the middle of the two end ranges you just experienced.

Although this may seem like a lot when reading it, these simple shoulder movements only take a few minutes to show to a classroom of people. Ask the students to notice where they are stuck and where they have the most movement in the above exercises. Once they connect with their shoulders, our focus can shift into teaching an awareness of a healthy posture rather than the "deskasana" position. We can start to bring about change by encouraging them to feel their shoulder blades firming onto their upper back, while at the same time widening through the collar bones and opening the chest. Tight pectoral muscles on the chest draw the shoulder blades out of a healthy alignment, so before asking students to practice Downward Dog and Sun Salutations, we must warm up their shoulders and open their chests, starting with warm-ups like the exercises above and moving into standing poses with varying arm positions.

To experience the importance of gently working the shoulders before doing Downward Dog, take a moment and mimic the "deskasana" posture. Stand with your shoulders rolled forward some, notice how the palms of your hands now face behind you. Feel your upper back rounding over. Now holding that slumped posture try and take your arms over your head as if you were going into Downward Dog. Did you get stuck part way? Most new students with a rounded posture like this will not be able to easily take their arms over their heads. This is why when we ask them to go into Downward Dog too early, their Dogs look rounded at their shoulders and they can't lengthen out their spines.

For these students, it is helpful to borrow some shoulder and chest warm-ups from Pilates and other fitness classes. There are many stretches to relax and open the front body. Although they can be done in many ways, my students enjoy working with foam rollers.

Practice: Foam Roller Shoulder Warm-up and Chest Opener

1. Place the foam roller in the center of your mat and parallel to the long sides. Sit on one end of the foam roller with your feet out to each side for balance and with the rest of the roller lying behind you.
2. Slowly lower yourself down onto your back, using your hands to help you. Feel your pelvis, your upper back, and the back of your head on the roller.
3. Take a moment here to relax and breathe, letting your hands and forearms rest on the floor on either side.
4. Bring your arms up towards the ceiling with your palms facing each other and begin to make small arm circles.
5. Work to keep your spine quiet as you increase the size of the circles, doing some each way. Notice how your shoulder blades move and "hug" the foam roller.
6. When your arms go out to the sides, keep your hands above shoulder height and make your inhales and exhales long and smooth.
7. After you finish some circles both ways, then once again bring your arms up towards the ceiling and directly above your shoulders with your palms facing each other.
8. Take an inhale to prepare. On the exhale, let your hands come out to either side until they are floating above the

floor at about the same height as your shoulders or a little higher.

9. Keeping your arms long and your hands elevated around shoulder height, imagine you are making snow angels in the air by slowly moving your arms up and down alongside your body. Feel the weight of your arms stretching and opening your chest.
10. Notice where your shoulders and chest feel the tightest, and pause in those places for a moment to breathe and let yourself open up.
11. To come off of the roller, gently roll to one side, using your hands to help you. Lie on your back for a few breaths and relax.

SHOULDER STRETCHES MIXED WITH THE STANDING POSES

Whenever I plan on teaching a shoulder-focused yoga session, I try to add in as many shoulder stretches and chest openers as possible early in the class. Many of the standing poses already warm and work the shoulders, and we can get creative by adding additional stretches. Some examples of this are Eagle arms in Warrior 2 or Goddess, Cow Face arms in the Warrior poses or Tree, or fingers clasped behind the back in any of these poses. I've seen yoga instructors be successful with many creative combinations. It all depends on who you have in the room and if they can safely do it.

Traditionally, the most common chest opening in the standing poses has been to clasp the fingers together behind the back in poses like Standing Forward Fold or Wide-Legged Forward Fold and then lift the hands away from the pelvis. This common cue is effective for opening the chest, and many teachers will have students breathe deeply into the chest while holding a forward bend with their hands behind their back. However, with some students their shoulders are so rolled forward that the traditional clasping of the hands behind is actually too much for them. In these cases, we can ask them to rest their hands on the back of their pelvis with their palms facing out and then cue them to try to widen through their collar bones. The same students who have trouble clasping their hands behind the back may also not be ready for too many forward bends. A better option for them would be to practice palms out on the back of the pelvis in the Warriors (mixed up with the traditional arm positions), and also in a gentle version of Locust.

Stretching the shoulders using a dowel is an option for students with less flexible shoulders and provides a different experience than using a yoga strap.

WORKING WITH A DOWEL TO OPEN THE SHOULDERS

Traditionally, yogis have used yoga straps to make shoulder stretches more accessible, but I've taken to using shorter dowels.[1] I prefer 2-foot dowels that are about an 1¾ inches thick. These are shorter and thicker than the longer dowels that are commonly used for different exercises and assists. These shorter dowels are nice, as students can grasp them and then imagine that they are pulling their hands away from each other or pressing towards one another creating different muscle engagements and stretches. Dowels can be used in all the warrior poses above the head, and in the standing forward bends with the dowel behind the back with the palms facing out (thumbs pointing towards each other).

Practice: Shoulder Stretches with a Dowel

1. While sitting in a comfortable position, take the dowel overhead slightly in front of you and grasp it with your hands, palms facing the front (thumbs in), a little wider than shoulder-width apart. Keep your elbows slightly bent.
2. Notice where you are holding your shoulders and make sure they are in a comfortable neutral position, not too far up by your ears (elevated) and not too far down your back (depressed) creating tension. You may need to lift your shoulders and shoulder blades up here a little if you have a habit of forcing them down, or release them down if you tend to hold them up towards your ears.
3. Wrap your fingers around the dowel and gently squeeze while pressing your hands towards each other.
4. As you hug in on the dowel, feel your biceps firm up with a feeling of wrapping towards your back body. Feel your underarms tone and hollow.
5. Keep toning your underarms and slowly move your arms back as far as you can comfortably, but no further than over the crown of your head. After a few breaths, bring the dowel back to where you started.
6. Now, pull your hands away from each other on the dowel and bend your spine to the right (side flexion). Take a few breaths and then move to the other side. Finish by coming upright again to the center.

7. Take the dowel in your right hand and then hold your hand behind your head so the dowel hangs behind you along your spine. Your right palm will be facing the back of your head. Keep your neck in line with your spine and avoid bowing your head forward.
8. Take your left arm out to the side with your thumb pointing towards the floor. Bend your elbow and see if you can slide the back of your left hand behind you, palm out, and try to grasp the bottom of the dowel. (If this isn't available to you, see #11 for a modification.)
9. If you can reach the dowel with the left hand, then grasp it and gently pull your hands away from each other on the dowel.
10. Walk your hands towards each other on the dowel, stopping every half inch or so to grasp the dowel and pull your hands gently away from each other. Take your time, and when you are ready, switch sides and repeat steps 6-10.
11. If the dowel doesn't work for you, then try this classic triceps stretch instead. Take both arms overhead, bend your right elbow and bring your right hand behind your head with the palm facing the back of your head. Then take your left hand and grasp your right wrist, forearm, or elbow (whichever you can reach comfortably). With your left hand, gently pull your right elbow towards the left for a triceps stretch on your right arm.

ALIGNING THE SHOULDERS IN STANDING POSES

With the standing poses, we have the opportunity to teach students how to stabilize their shoulder blades in a healthy alignment without the stress of weight bearing. Clear cueing for the shoulders is just as important in Triangle as it is in Handstand. The poses will become more stable and the shoulders safer when we can connect with the feeling of energy moving from the feet through the core into the shoulder blades, and out to the fingertips and even to the back of the head.

In poses such as Triangle, Side Angle, and Half Moon, students often let the hand that is raised above them move back behind them, causing pinching at the back of the shoulder. There are two different reasons we may find students in this misalignment. First, those who have flexible shoulders let the arm flop back behind them while at the same time attempting to look at the ceiling. For these students, we need to encourage them to bring their arm and hand directly above their shoulder and then firm up the muscles around their shoulder blades and also the arms. We can also remind them that looking at the ceiling is not required, as getting the shoulder aligned is the first priority.

The second example of this misalignment is students who are tighter in the shoulders and chest but still try to force their way into the pose. These students cannot rotate the upper chest easily, but they try to look up at the ceiling anyway, kinking their neck and forcing their raised arm behind them. For these students, we can ask them to soften and relax, suggesting that they back off and find more comfort in the pose. Again, we will ask them to bring the raised hand directly above the shoulder, and for now let go of trying to look up at the ceiling. If their shoulders are less flexible, then they may be more comfortable with their raised hand slightly in front of their body or placed on the hip.

In Warrior 1 with the arms overhead, it is helpful to offer students the option to keep their hands slightly forward of their shoulders, if needed. As we discussed earlier in this chapter, taking the hands directly over the head may not be an option, and it may also be uncomfortable. Cueing them to take their arms out to each side in a T position first, and then turn palms up and continue lifting overhead from there, is often easier anatomically for people than trying to lift their arms up in front of them.

Beginners also often overuse their upper trapezius and other muscles in the neck when holding up their arms. Teachers try many cues to encourage students to stop this common habit of tensing the shoulders up by the ears. Some cues like "let your shoulders release down your back," or "soften the tops of your shoulders away from your ears" are a good start. After we hopefully convince them to release the tension in their neck and shoulders, we then need to guide them to firm the muscles around the shoulder blades that do a more effective job at holding up the arms. One cue I've always loved is to ask students to "imagine they are holding their arms up from the backs of their hearts." It directs their attention to in-between and around their shoulders blades where I want them to firm up the muscles. Another cue I like to try is, "magnetize your shoulder blades onto your back."

WORKING WITH THE SHOULDERS IN SIDE ANGLE

In Side Angle, many of the alignment issues discussed above come into play. Students with flexible shoulders and backs send the top hand behind them, creating a backbend. For these students we can ask them to bring their biceps directly over their ears and firm the muscles around the shoulder blades. Those with less flexible shoulders struggle to get their arm above the head and often bend the elbow and internally rotate the arm to compensate. In this case, it is better to have them place their top hand on their hip and keep the shoulder safe.

The elevation/depression exercise from the warm-up earlier in this chapter can be briefly reviewed when focusing on the placement of the top shoulder blade in Side Angle. Some students bring their shoulder way up towards their ears, while others press the blade down the back to the end of their ROM. We can ask the students to find a comfortable place somewhere in the middle, where they can comfortably take their arm overhead. If the blade is too far down the back, then the arm will not go overhead. If you are not sure what I mean, take a moment to firm your shoulder blades as far down your back as you can, and then try and bring your arms overhead. Most people get stuck, especially if they lift their arms in front of them because our shoulders are not designed to work that way. This fundamental concept applies not only to Side Angle but also to all the poses where we take our arms overhead.

Practice: Side Angle

1. Take a comfortable wide stance facing the long side of your mat.
2. Pivoting on your right heel, turn your right hip out, letting your knees and toes follow. Your pelvis will also turn some to the right as you pivot.
3. Pivot on your left big toe mound and turn your left hip in a little, again letting the knee follow. Your left heel will be a little farther back than your big toe mound.
4. Check in with your left knee and adjust your hip position if needed in order to keep the knee happy.
5. Place your heels in a line or a little wider.
6. Ground into your outer heels and your big toe mounds, drawing energy into your arches and up into your legs and hips.
7. Bend your right knee and while keeping your torso long, fold at your right hip until you can place your right forearm onto your right thigh.
8. Press your right forearm into your right thigh and engage your core as you lengthen your whole right side. Avoid dumping all your weight into your right forearm and shoulder.
9. Rather than trying to stack your hips, let your pelvis stay where it naturally arrived as you came into the pose. Your left hip pointer will likely be a little forward of your right hip pointer.
10. Draw your hip pointers towards each other while firming

your abdominals and zip up your low belly from pubic bone to belly button.

11. Let your left hand hang in front of you for a moment with your palm facing you. Then, bring your shoulder blade into a comfortable position, not too far up near the ear, nor shoved all the way down your back.
12. From there, bend your elbow and bring your thumb towards your underarm, and then send your hand past your ear and overhead with your biceps near your ears. Stretch your left arm long over your head while imagining your shoulder blade is magnetized to your torso. Let the little finger side of your hand rotate towards the floor.
13. While grounding down into the left outer heel and big toe mound, feel the energy moving into your foot and all the way through to your left fingertips, creating a long line with the left side of your body.
14. Imagine you are working the thighs away from each other as if you are gently trying to stretch your mat a little longer with your feet.
15. If you want to look up, then firm your low right belly to stabilize your pelvis and gently rotate your ribs towards the left so your sternum is moving towards the ceiling. Let your head and gaze follow the rotation of the ribs.
16. If you feel any discomfort in your hips, your SI joints, or your adductor attachments when you attempt the rotation and upward gaze, then take the rotation out and simply look straight ahead. Another option is to try looking down at your right thigh.
17. Feel the breath moving the ribs while you continue to ground your feet and lengthen your side.
18. To come out of the pose, reverse the rotation first, soften your knees, and then as you come up to standing, work your legs gently away from each other while imagining that you are trying to make your mat a little longer.

TEACHING DOWNWARD DOG

For many beginners, Downward Dog is a difficult pose to enjoy, and so we need to be careful as teachers not to refer to it as a "resting pose." After we get into yoga, we learn to like Downward Dog, but it is an acquired taste. As we have discussed above, new students often have shoulder issues and unhealthy postural habits that contribute to them not liking Downward Dog, and they also lack sufficient upper body strength. In my own practice, now that my shoulders and chest are open, the Downward Dog is all about elongating my spine, especially my low back. Lengthening and strengthening my back in the pose keeps my back and hips from hurting. I love to watch students over a period of time lengthen out in this pose. They will go from looking tight, tense, and bent, to appearing relaxed and long as their ribs move slowly with the breath.

Once the shoulders are warmed up and students are ready to lift up into the Downward Dog, we need to remind them to ground all the fingers and knuckle pads into the mat, not just the outside (pinky side) of the hand that they tend to gravitate towards. We want to incorporate putting weight on the thumb and pointer finger pad too, as this is where the bone structure is better designed to hold the weight. In addition, if we engage and spread the weight over the whole hand, we are more likely to use muscles on both sides of the arm. Many students, especially women, do not engage their biceps at all in this pose; by pressing into the whole hand and gently hugging the forearms towards each other, we can begin to get all the muscles integrated.

If students have a tight lower back, less flexible hamstrings, or both, then it's best to have them bend their knees in the posture. Bending the knees in the posture is not traditional, but if the back of their body is tight then the pressure will go somewhere along the back body and potentially create an injury or make one worse. For example, students who are tight along the entire back line of their body will have a flexed low back in Downward Dog if they don't bend their knees.

This has the potential to create or aggravate disc problems with some students, just as we discussed above with standing and seated forward bending. Often these same students also have less flexible hamstrings, and when they straighten their legs it can cause too much pulling at the hamstring attachment sites. Even with the knees bent, they are still stretching the hamstrings, but the chance for hamstring attachment injuries is reduced. With the pressure off the hamstrings and low back, the students can focus on elongating their backs and opening the shoulders.

At the beginning of learning the practice, many students will not be able to get their arms straight over their heads, or their biceps anywhere near their ears in Downward Dog. Sometimes their shoulders will look like they are at an angle. It takes time for the chest and shoulders to open up, and so we should *not force* students into the position by pressing on their backs or shoulders. We can just ask them to shift back as far as they can comfortably. If we continue to offer shoulder stretches and chest openers, then most students will eventually straighten out in their own time.

Practice: Downward Dog

1. Starting on hands and knees, bring your hands about shoulder-width apart and spread your fingers out. Press evenly into the pads of your fingertips and knuckles as well as the heel of your hands.
2. Imagine the center of your palms lifting up and energy moving upwards into your arms and shoulders (see the Integrating the Whole Hand section of Chapter 9 for clarity on this cue).
3. Curl your toes under and lift your pelvis up into the air, lengthening your back.
4. If you are less flexible in your legs, hips, or shoulders, try bending your knees as much as necessary to get comfortable. If you are more flexible, then straighten your legs the best you can without rounding your back.

5. Feel the breath moving your ribs as you zip up and tone your low belly.
6. Firm your thighs and gently hug your forearms towards each other, engaging your biceps.
7. Once you feel your muscles engaged, shift your torso back towards your legs as your body allows, letting your heels gently drop down towards the mat. There is no need to force the heels to the floor here; go slowly until you feel a stretch in your calves.
8. If you are flexible, then don't let your torso sink too far down and create a backbend.
9. Focus on getting your neck in line with your spine. As your shoulders open up, your head will eventually be between your arms or somewhere near.
10. Imagine you are making the side of your waists longer, lifting your pelvis up away from your ribs and elongating your lower back.
11. Keep gently hugging your forearms towards each other and energetically lift the center of your palms as you hollow out your underarms.
12. As you inhale, send your breath in between your shoulder blades behind your heart and feel a sensation of your blades and muscles wrapping around to the side of your body.
13. Elongate your back by reaching your pelvis one way and the crown of your head the other.
14. To come out of the pose, bend your knees and bring them to the mat. Shift back into Pose of the Child and rest.

MODIFIED SUN SALUTATIONS

For many students, a Sun Salutation is the first set of postures they learn and recognize. In popular flow classes around the country, it is not uncommon for teachers to offer twenty or more Sun Salutations. Unfortunately, for new students this is often way too many for a safe start, especially if they arrive with rolled forward shoulders and posture issues as we have been discussing. If we went to an experienced personal trainer and told them that we hadn't been working out and didn't have much strength in our upper body, they would start us out with low weights and fewer repetitions. Although practicing numerous Sun Salutations has been part of the tradition many of us have learned in yoga, it is worth rethinking, and it would help many of our students if we introduced repetitions of Sun Salutations more slowly. Giving students the option of resting in Pose of the Child is a start, but we need to give people the option of continuing to move with the class if they want. No matter how many Sun Salutations we sequence in our flows, we can offer modifications and options for students to continue working without hurting their shoulders as they gain strength and improve their posture. For more sequencing options for Sun Salutations, see the Reducing Wrist Pain section in Chapter 9.

The first, and probably most important, modification is to take lowering into the full Four-Limbed Staff (Chaturanga Dandasana) out of the sequence. Four-limbed Staff is a difficult posture to hold with safe shoulder alignment. Beginners who have not been doing push-ups regularly let their shoulders roll forward lower than their elbows while gripping their upper trapezius and other neck muscles. In an attempt to float through to Upward Dog, they put their shoulders at risk as they roll forward with this unhealthy alignment. Rotator cuff attachment injuries are common in people over 40 no matter what type of exercise they do, but these poorly executed Four-Limbed Staff poses are probably one of the biggest sources of shoulder injuries in yoga. One possible modification is to have students put their knees down and then lower all the way to the floor while focusing on keeping the shoulder blades firmly on the back and keeping the chest and collarbones wide and open. Once on the floor, place the hands in position for either Cobra or Upward Dog and press up into the backbend from the floor. Another option would be to flow between a high plank and Downward Dog a few times and wait to do the backbends in a later sequence. I teach stronger students before and after classes how to properly do Four-Limbed Staff if they want to include it, and then during public mixed classes I offer one of the above modifications.

Another change we can make is to have students step forward and backward into and out of low lunges instead of the traditional hopping forward and backward. Jumping from standing forward fold to Four-Limbed Staff is certainly fun for those who are strong enough, but this is an advanced move that many students will never be able to do well. Most new students dump into their low backs when they jump back, and some of them also let their shoulder blades "wing" up. They don't have enough strength yet to keep their shoulder blades stable on their back.[2] Adding in the lunges makes the whole sequence more accessible to beginners, while also stretching their hip flexors. For those who have trouble swinging their foot up between their hands for the low lunges, have them put one knee down first and then bring their other foot forward, even using the hand to help get that foot up in position.

POSITIONAL AWARENESS AND STABILIZATION OF THE SHOULDER BLADES

While learning Downward Dog and Sun Salutations, many students gain strength and quickly learn to hold their shoulder blades in a comfortable, stable position. There are a subset of students though who struggle with this fundamental. In poses where the arms bear weight such as Plank, Side Plank, Downward Dog, and Dolphin, they have a habit of holding their shoulder blades either too close to the ears or too far down the back. One way to help students build positional awareness of their shoulders is to try the elevation and depression exercise we covered earlier, but to cue it upside down in the Dolphin. If they tend to grip in their upper trapezius, sending their shoulder blades toward their ears, then in Dolphin their heads will lift up and contract their neck and shoulders, like a turtle taking its head into its shell. If they have a habit of shoving their shoulder blades down their back and creating tension in both the neck and mid back, then in Dolphin their head will come out of the turtle shell and be either too close to the floor or resting on the floor. Students can practice moving their shoulder blades up and down their backs and find a neutral position that works for them, where they are the most comfortable. Once they have found their best neutral position, the next step is to learn to keep their blades stable in the poses. This is a particularly important fundamental for students to master before they attempt inversions (more on readiness for inversions in Chapter 10).

Practice: Elevation and Depression in Dolphin

1. Starting on hands and knees, bring your forearms to the mat and clasp your fingers together.
2. Curl your toes under and lift your pelvis up in the air.
3. If your back or hamstrings are less flexible, bend your knees.
4. Walk your feet in towards your elbows while keeping your thighs engaged and your belly firm.
5. Bring your pelvis directly over your shoulders, or as close to that as you can.
6. Gently press your elbows into the mat and hug your forearms towards each other, firming your biceps.
7. Imagine you are drawing eggs into your underarms, hollowing your armpits.
8. Keep breathing steadily into your ribs.
9. Lift your heels up and see if you can walk your toes in a little closer to your head.
10. Notice where you are holding your head: is it drawn up into your body, resting on the floor, or in the middle of these two extremes?
11. Try to move your shoulder blades slowly up and down your back and notice your range of motion.
12. Find a comfortable middle place for your shoulders, and magnetize your shoulder blades onto your torso.

13. To come out of the pose, walk your feet back some, bring your knees to the mat, and rest in Pose of the Child.

Strengthen + Stretch + Awareness

In summary, to help our students maintain healthy strong shoulders for life, we need to start first with educating them about their posture and urging them to stop practicing "deskasana." With this also comes education about how their shoulders work and safe ways to stretch and strengthen them. Our mixed level classes need to include chest openers and upper back strengtheners to support the creation of a healthier posture. Through the poses we can encourage our students to connect with and stabilize their shoulders, and with this awareness they will move in a more integrated and healthy way throughout their day.

9
SUPPORTING THE WRISTS, HANDS, AND ELBOWS

We heavily depend on our hands and wrists at work every day, no matter what our job is or what our daily activities entail. Typing on a keyboard or texting on a phone puts stress on our hands. Jobs such as bartender, server, hair stylist, massage therapist, salesclerk, and many others also require strength and repetitive motions. When new students come into class, we don't know what they've been doing all day, and we have no idea if they have weak or strong hands and wrists. Just like everything else in the yoga room, we have to strike a balance between relaxing the hands and wrists and strengthening and stretching them.

Many of the modifications and sequencing issues we talked about for the shoulders in Chapter 8 also apply here. Poses where we bear weight on the shoulders also include a lot of work for the wrists and hands. Wrist pain is a common complaint for students new to yoga. If they try to do too much too soon, they may inflame the wrists. This will cause them to have to rest and perhaps even stop yoga for a number of weeks to let their wrists recover. As teachers, we need to guide and encourage students to start slowly with the poses where weight is placed on the hands and wrists, and to impart the wisdom of experience that paying attention to how the wrists feel during and after practice is very important.

Students at our studio who arrive with wrist, shoulder, and neck pain from their jobs often become pain free over a period of months with an accessible yoga practice. This will happen naturally and organically for many students if we model a gentle start to practice and use common sense. I've also seen students who have become competitive and ego driven hurt their wrists in an attempt to get into too many hand balances too soon. All I can do is keep repeating that they need to back off, and that I don't think they have the core strength yet to do those poses.

In this chapter, we will also cover how to recognize hyperextension of the elbow. With so many hypermobile people attracted to yoga, it is important for us as instructors to recognize hyperextension and know how to guide students into a healthier alignment of the elbow joint. In addition, we will also discuss two different structural issues that many teachers confuse: hyperextension of the elbow and the carrying angle of the elbow. It is common for teachers to give students a cue to address hyperextension when in fact the students are not hyperextending and just have a large carrying angle.

REDUCING WRIST PAIN WITH NEW STUDENTS

Not only does the emphasis on Sun Salutations and Downward Dog create shoulder issues, as we've discussed in Chapter 8, it also contributes to wrist discomfort. We can tell students' wrists are bothering them when they try to compensate by lifting their palms up and then moving to their fingertips or fists. If we give students time to build up wrist strength and incorporate some wrist and finger stretches into our practice, many people will be able to tolerate at least some Downward Dogs and high planks.

Since so many of us teach mixed level classes, it is hard to include all the Sun Salutations that the regular students want and enjoy while also helping a beginner get safely started. Creating an environment where it is understood that all the Sun Salutations are optional is helpful. As new students come into the mixed level class, take a moment to tell them that they do not need to do all the Sun Salutations at first and advise them to only do some the first day and slowly work into all of them over a few months. As I mentioned in Chapter 8, offer options for other poses or exercises to do other than Sun Salutations, and not just Pose of the Child. Suggest to students that during the Sun Salutations, they are free to choose what works for them and then have everyone meet back in Downward Dog. Someone who wants a workout could choose to hold a forearm Plank or a Dolphin - giving their wrists a rest, while another person might choose Locust. Creating this type of environment not only reduces competition, which can lead to injury, but it also encourages students to take responsibility for themselves.

For Sun Salutations, we have a number of options to offer those with acute wrist problems. The first is having them do a modified version with a chair. For Downward Dog have students place their hands on the seat of a chair and then walk their feet back under the hips. For lunges ask them to hold onto the sides of the chair seat with the hands slightly forward of their shoulders. Leave the backbend out of the sequencing when using the chair, as students tend to dump into their low back when they try it. I've successfully integrated students with wrist problems into my classes this way; the only time they need the chair is for Sun Salutations, and then they put it to the side. Another option is to have the student practice a variation of the Sun Salutation on their forearms. Have them go from Dolphin to forearm plank, and then lower down onto their belly for Cobra. Working from the forearms is a little awkward at first, but students work it out, and they can still get the shoulder and core strengthening they want without irritating their wrists.

Integrating the Whole Hand

Another way to teach students to take pressure off their wrists in weight-bearing poses is to have them press equally into both sides of the hand, the large knuckle pads, and all of the fingers. With the whole hand active, the muscles on both sides of the arm are encouraged to participate. When we press into the thumb side of the hand, the biceps and inner arm muscles firm with energy radiating into the chest. When we press into the pinky side of the hand, the triceps and outer arm muscles firm with energy moving into the muscles of the upper back. Obviously, we want both sides of the arm to help support us when bearing weight on the hands, but it takes some work and reminding to consistently get new students to do this.

Part of the struggle for students with tight shoulders is that it is not always comfortable for them to press the thumb pads and pointer fingers down. It's more comfortable to just roll to the outside of the hand. For these students, allowing them to turn their arms and hands out slightly in Downward Dog may give them just enough relief to get the pointer finger pressed into the mat. Over time as the shoulders open and if it works for them, they can move the arms and wrists to the more traditional position of the wrist creases parallel to the front of the mat. Although my shoulders are flexible, I sometimes have trouble keeping my biceps engaged, and turning my arms and hands out ever so slightly is all the adjustment I need to get more integrated in the pose.

In any class I teach, there will be at least a few new students rolling onto the outside of the hands and letting the large knuckle pads of the pointer fingers and the thumb pads pop up, so I frequently cue them to spread out the fingers and press all the fingers and large knuckle pads into the mat. Not only does this help engage all the muscles of the arms and shoulders as we've discussed, it also helps protect the pinky side of the hand. When students roll to the outside of their hands in Downward Dog, they put a lot of unneeded stress on the smaller bones of the ulnar side of the hand. This often aggravates any issues students have from computer work. The ulnar nerve and artery run through the wrist on the pinky side, and this is where people tend to rest their hands at the keyboard or mouse.[1]

Think of the palms of the hands like the arches of our feet. We lift our arches to draw energy up into the legs and hips. In poses with weight on the hands, we can imagine that we are drawing energy from our palms into our arms and shoulders and even into our upper back. Imagine you have a rose petal under your palm, and you are trying not to crush it, while still grounding into the fingertips and large knuckle pads. For an example of when to use this cue, see the Downward Dog practice in Chapter 8. For those who have trouble breaking the habit of dumping all the weight onto the wrist, try placing a big car wash sponge behind each wrist, so that when the student comes into Downward Dog, the arm comes down and squishes the sponge. This creates a little feeling of lifting up or support at the heel of the hand while sending some weight forward into the palms and fingers.

Working with Less Flexible or Sore Wrists and Hands

The hands and shoulders affect each other. When one is less flexible or out of alignment, it is often felt up or down the arm as pain, soreness, or numbness. We hold a lot of tension in our hands. We use them constantly, and depending on our daily required tasks, this tension can go from soreness to intense pain quickly. Students who use their hands all day long at work may come to class with tight or sore wrists and fingers. If they have arthritis forming in their hands or have been developing symptoms of inflammation, such as carpal tunnel syndrome, then they may need to avoid Downward Dog and Sun Salutations for a while. However, in some cases a small number of modified Sun Salutations, done slowly, actually help students with wrist and hand issues. When new students come to my classes presenting with these issues, I advise them to start slowly and pay attention to how their hands and wrists feel, not only during class but also a few days after.

It is helpful to begin class with breath work combined with hand movements. Inhale as the fingers extend and stretch, and then on the exhale let the fingers curl and the hands feel heavy and relaxed. After encouraging awareness of the hands, we can then begin adding gentle wrist, finger, and palm stretches into our classes. Another way to start class is by rolling out the hands with tennis balls or smaller little rubber balls. This feels good and effectively releases tension in the hands and all the way up into the shoulders. Even just brushing the fingers of one hand with the other hand and then gently pulling on them often creates a feeling of relaxation.

With the reverse namaste hand position it is best to start slowly with the wrists higher than the elbows.

Towards the end of class and after including weight-bearing poses on the hands, it's nice to stretch the wrists in the opposite direction than they've been working. The classical wrist stretch where yogis stand on the palms of the hands is often used after hand balances, but it is not accessible to everyone and can hurt.

A gentler option is to bring the hands to Anjali Mudra (prayer hands), and then while keeping the fingers pointing upward turn the hands around to bring the backs of the hands together (reverse prayer hands).

Due to differences in students' wrists, the backs of the hands may not come together entirely, and they may need to adjust the height of their hands or elbows. Once the hands are in a comfortable position, round the upper back a little and lower the wrists towards the navel until a gentle stretch is felt. Be careful not to side bend the wrists trying to place the hands together. When I do this stretch, I like to intertwine my fingers, squeezing them together gently.

Strengthening Hands and Wrists for Weight-Bearing Poses

As mentioned above the key here is to go slowly and give the wrists and hands time to build up strength. When Sun Salutations are appropriate, start these students with a small number of Downward Dogs and Planks and see if their wrists can tolerate it. If so, then ask them to try two to six Sun Salutations the next class, depending on their regular activity and fitness level. Give them permission to build up the repetitions over a period of months. The older the student, the more caution needs to be taken when teaching Downward Dog and Sun Salutations, as many older wrists will not tolerate an abundance of weight bearing. For those who need to gain basic strength, additional hand exercises can be helpful: squeezing a rubber ball, or the opposite action of placing a rubber band around all the fingers and thumb and then stretching it out as the fingers open.

For those working towards Sun Salutations and inversions, consider adding other ways to strengthen the wrists rather than just adding more repetitions of Sun Salutations. Weightlifting is always a great option, but I also love my pull-up bar. I have a pull-up bar with three different hand hold positions that I hang on. Although I'm not great at pull-ups, I can hang and bring my knees up and down for some core work. This strengthens the wrists in a different position than when on the yoga mat.

BREAKING THE PATTERN OF HYPEREXTENSION

For as long as I can remember, I've been able to hyperextend my elbows, making my arms look rather broken from certain angles. When I was younger it didn't bother me much, but as I got older, I would get an uncomfortable pinching feeling in the elbow while weight bearing. When I first started yoga, teachers would tell me to soften my elbows, but at first I couldn't feel the difference between a truly straight arm and a crooked hyperextended arm. When I heard the word "straight," I would automatically hyperextend my elbows. Although teachers continued to correct me, I didn't really know how to fix it.

Over time, I began to understand through my practice what a straight arm truly meant versus what felt straight to me in my body. In order to get stronger and not irritate my elbows I had to think of bending my elbows while at the same time hugging my forearms towards each other. If I bent and hugged in, then my biceps would engage. In my mind, I thought I was bending my elbows a lot, but when someone took a picture of me, I could see they were only slightly bent. Even though I can still hyperextend some even now, once my biceps developed and my elbow joints were more stable, my elbows quit hurting. What helped me was a combination of joint awareness and alignment, and then strengthening the surrounding muscles.

In every classroom, there will be a least a handful of students (mostly women) who are not using their biceps much at all. Whether they hyperextend or not, we want students using all the muscles on both sides of their arms for weight bearing. I like to use a dowel in Dolphin to begin the process of awareness.

Practice: Dolphin with a Dowel

1. Start in Table with the dowel in front of you on the floor.
2. Come down onto your forearms with your elbows about shoulder-width apart, and place the dowel in your hands with your palms up. Gently press your elbows and forearms into the mat.
3. Wrap your fingers around the dowel firmly, and then isometrically draw your hands towards each other on the dowel. Feel your biceps firm up and your underarms lift up and hollow out as the muscles in the upper back tone.
4. Curl your toes under and lift your pelvis in the air.
5. Tone your low belly and draw your hip pointers toward each other.
6. Begin walking your toes as close to your head as is comfortable. If your hamstrings or back are uncomfortable, then try bending your knees.
7. Keep isometrically drawing your hands towards each other on the dowel as you bring your pelvis as close to directly above your shoulders as you can. Pause here to take a few breaths into your ribs as you work on keeping both sides of your arms active.
8. To come out of the pose, lower your knees down and shift back into Pose of the Child. Release the dowel and stretch your arms out and breathe.

This same technique of isometrically drawing in the forearms can be used to awaken the biceps in other poses where the weight is on the shoulders, such as Downward Dog, Upward Dog, and Plank. In all of these poses, students who hyperextend also sometimes swing the eyes of their elbows (the center crease of the inside elbow) around to the front of the pose (facing their fingers), making it even harder for them to keep their biceps toned. Ask these students to try to keep the eyes of their elbows more in line with their thumbs. We want to avoid cueing exact angles here as the joints vary in students. Some teachers suggest that students face the eyes of the elbows toward each other or toward the midline of the mat, but for many students this causes pinching and compression near the glenohumeral joint.

Using a dowel is a great teaching tool to help students learn to engage their biceps in Dolphin. Once learning this fundamental in Dolphin they will hopefully apply it also in poses like Downward Dog and Side Plank.

In Upward Dog, we can watch students for hyperextension and placement of the eyes of the elbow. Bending the elbows is helpful in this pose, not only to encourage muscle engagement if they hyperextend, but also to help them deepen the backbend in the upper back.

Practice: Upward Dog

1. Start by lying on your belly. Elongate your spine and reach your legs long. Firm your thighs and tone your glutes without clenching them together.
2. Bring your palms onto the mat about shoulder-width apart,

placing them near your ribs, a little below your shoulders.

3. Bow your head some and tone the front of your throat. Widen your collarbones and feel your shoulders lift up slightly.
4. Firm your belly by drawing your hip pointers together and zipping up the front of the pelvis.
5. Keeping your knees down, lead with your chest as you press your torso, including your pelvis, off the mat. Let your head and gaze be the last thing to come up.
6. You can lift your knees off the mat for the traditional Upward Dog if you like or leave your knees down.
7. Bend your elbows slightly and gently hug your forearms towards each other, firming your biceps. Feel your chest lift upward and the muscles in your upper back firm.
8. Keep your elbows in line with your shoulders. Don't let them splay out.
9. Bring your breath into your back low ribs, continuing to tone your belly as you let the upper backbend develop.
10. If you would like to go into Downward Dog, then start by drawing your belly in and up, and then turn your toes under and take your pelvis up and back into the pose.
11. To come out of the pose, keep your belly toned as you bring your knees to the mat, then shift back and take a few breaths in Pose of the Child.

Rotating Elbow Issues in Upward Dog

Before correcting hyperextension issues in Upward Dog, we need to walk around to the front of the mat where the student's hands are planted to get a complete view of the situation. If we see the eyes of the elbows facing the front, then this is a student that hyperextends while also laterally rotating their humerus (swinging the eyes of the elbows towards the front). We need to help the student correct the elbow position first. Suggest placing the eyes of the elbows in line with the thumbs, then ask the student to soften the elbows a little. It often takes a while for students to come into awareness of how they are holding their elbows. Give people some time to integrate the information. Instead of correcting them every time you see them, gently remind them every few weeks or months. This teaching tip also applies to Downward Dog, Plank, and Side Plank.

ELBOW POSITION IN FOUR-LIMBED STAFF (CHATURANGA)

In Four-Limbed Staff, there are a variety of opinions about where to hold the elbows, and this causes confusion. However, everyone seems to agree that we shouldn't let students splay their elbows way out to the side. One popular cue that some teachers like to say, "hug your elbows into your ribs," works for some students and not for others. The difference in how the cue is received lies in anatomical differences of the students. The cue works for those students who have wider rib cages that are shaped more like a square. In this case, their ribs extend to their sides at around the same width as their shoulders. It doesn't work for students who have wide shoulders and narrow rib cages. When students with a smaller rib cage, wide shoulders, and a long humerus 'hug' the elbows to their rib cage, it puts an incredible amount of pressure on the upper trapezius at the base of the neck. For these students this cue could cause neck issues over time and may also put too much pressure on the rotator cuff muscles. In private sessions, we can certainly use the cue to hug the elbows in with our barrel-chested students, especially if they don't have long arms. In a group class, it makes better sense to just say "keep your elbows in line with your shoulders" and let the students work out for themselves if that is touching their ribs or not.

HYPEREXTENSION VS. THE CARRYING ANGLE OF THE ELBOW

Many new fitness and yoga instructors confuse the carrying angle of the elbow with hyperextension. Most students coming into my trainings have never heard of the carrying angle of the elbow, and so the misunderstanding is not a surprise. It confuses students who know they are not hyperextending but can't figure out why the teacher is correcting them. This concept should be taught in every 200-hour training, as the incorrect adjustments to students cause a lot of frustration. First, let's look at the anatomical differences, and then how to discern the difference in poses.

Hyperextension of the elbow is when a person fully extends their arm, and the elbow joint continues to extend past where the arm would look straight. The elbow 'locks out' and it looks like it is moving in the opposite direction that it is designed to bend.

The carrying angle of the elbow represents an entirely different angle. When standing in the anatomical position with our arms at our sides and our palms are facing forward, the carrying angle is what causes the forearms and hands to be slightly farther from the body than the upper arm. Our arms are designed this way so that when we walk, our hands don't hit our hips or our legs. The angle between the forearm and the upper arm is usually measured between 5 and 15 degrees. When people have arms that are angled greater than 15 degrees, their arms look bent or crooked from certain angles, and then straight from other angles. This can lead teachers to become confused and think students are hyperextending.

Most studies show the carrying angle as slightly larger in the dominant hand for both men and women, and slightly larger in general for women.[2] However, this angle does not affect asana or people's abilities in sports. Attempts to move the hands further apart in Handstand or Downward Dog won't change the carrying angle and can put more pressure than necessary on the outer shoulders. Those with a very large carrying angle may struggle some while learning Handstand because their hands will plant forward of their shoulders.

This can be addressed by just turning out the arms and hands slightly (lateral rotation), with the hands still around shoulder-width apart, to make a bigger "base" for Handstand. In general though, students really do not need any modifications for a large carrying angle. This angle is determined by our bones; we are born with it, and it cannot be changed or "fixed".[3]

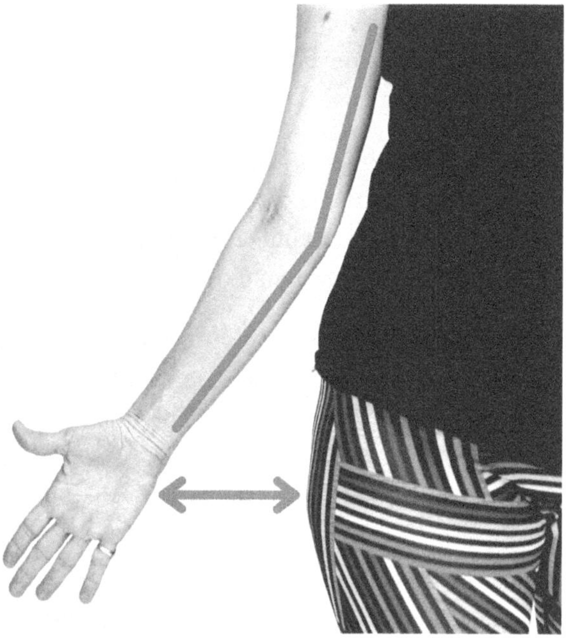

The carrying angle of the elbow determines how far the forearm and hand will be from the body.

Let's look at how we, as teachers, tell the difference between hyperextension and the carrying angle in a few poses. If a student is in Downward Dog and their arms look crooked, then we need to look at their pose from the front of their mat where their hands are planted, in order to see if they are hyperextending. From the front of their mat, we can clearly see if their elbows are extending past where their arms look straight. We can also note if the eyes of their elbows have moved around to face the front of the mat. To check if they have a deeper carrying angle, we need to walk to the side of the mat where we can see the whole pose. If their forearms seem closer to the floor and at a different angle than their humerus, then we are seeing the carrying angle. We can't always be sure if they are hyperextending from the side view. It is best to walk around to the front of the pose.

Walk around to the front of the pose when checking for hyperextension of the elbow in Downward Dog. From the front we can see the elbow joint clearly.

In standing poses like Triangle, we also need to walk around the pose before making a correction. In Triangle, we can see hyperextension better at the front of their mats, and the carrying angle better while viewing from the long side of their mats. However, students can trick us by rotating the upper arm in an unexpected position, so when unsure, look for the eye of the elbow or the point of the elbow for reference.

Over the years, many students have shown up at our studio frustrated because teachers continue to tell them they are hyperextending, when they feel they are not. In all of these cases, the student has a large carrying angle. In addition, these students can't figure out why their arms always look crooked in photographs when they know they are straightening their arms out as much as they possibly can. Students are visibly relieved when I tell them that it's just their carrying angle. They are made that way, and it's nothing they are doing wrong. One teacher in training burst into tears when she learned about her large carrying angle. She recalled a high school athletics coach who yelled at her continually to straighten her arms, and no matter how much effort she put into it, she couldn't make him happy.[4]

View Downward Dog from the long side of the mat to determine if you are seeing a larger carrying angle. In this photo the woman in front has a larger carrying angle.

THE FINGERS IN STANDING POSTURES

When I first started learning yoga, I noticed that yoga teachers from different styles emphasized different finger positions in the standing postures. Some yogis kept their fingers together in the standing poses, others liked to spread them apart as far as possible, and some didn't mention it all. I always wanted to know why a teacher was asking for something specific or making a correction, especially when it felt fine either way for me. I remember being corrected to both extremes, and I was mystified watching a woman work her fingers so much that it looked like she had claws.

I took it to my own mat and experimented with which way I liked better. What I concluded is that what goes on with the fingers isn't nearly as important as what is happening in the shoulders. First, we need to focus on helping students get their shoulders in a safe and comfortable position, and then they can choose how to hold their fingers.

In my own practice, I like to feel the sensation of energy drawing into my palms, up into my arms, and then into the muscles around my shoulders and upper back. I can engage or draw in my palms with my fingers spread out or pressed together, and I change up my hand positions depending on the pose. In Side Angle, I like the feeling created by bringing the fingers of my top arm together gently. This creates a long line of energy from my back heel through my fingertips. I like turning the pinky side of my top hand a little towards the floor to help engage the bicep. In many of the standing poses, I like to imagine that my arms are filled with helium balloons, and these same balloons are under my palms helping to hold my arms and hands up.[5] Another option, while the palms remain down, is to imagine palming small lightweight play balls, and let the thumb and pinky relax down with the center of the palm lifted to "hold" the ball under my hands. For grounding my hand in standing poses like Triangle, I find that being on my fingertips work best. I feel the energy lifting into the palms, rather than dumping down into the wrists.

When teaching, we should focus on guiding healthy shoulder positions and let the hands be the students' choice. Something in the middle of the two extremes will be the most comfortable for most people. Though suggestions on options for how to hold the hands are always helpful, rules are not really needed.

Putting It All Together with Side Plank

One challenging pose for the hands and wrists is Side Plank, and many students need to start practicing this pose first on their forearms to gain strength. When they are ready to go from the forearms to the hands, it is important for them to evenly press into the whole hand, including the fingertips and the large knuckle pads, along with imagining an energetic lift from the center of the palms. We can remind students to stay grounded into their thumb pads and the large knuckle pad of their pointer finger to avoid dumping all of the weight onto the outside of their wrists.

Practice: Side Plank

1. Starting in a high plank, press evenly through the palms and take some weight into the fingertips and thumbs.
2. Feel the center of your palms gently lift while you firm your shoulder blades onto your back.
3. Wrap your hip pointers towards each other as you draw your low belly in and up.
4. Breathe wide to the side into your ribs and relax your jaw.
5. Keeping that feeling of wrapping and firming through the low belly, bring your pelvis in line with your spine. Make a long line with your whole body, from heels to head.
6. Move your right hand a little bit forward of your shoulder and shift your weight onto your right hand as you roll onto the pinky toe side of your right foot.
7. Bring your left hand to your hip while you stack your left foot on top of your right and firm your thighs and glutes.
8. If this is too challenging right now, then bend your left knee and plant your left foot in front of you for support.
9. If you know that you sometimes hyperextend your elbows, then soften your right elbow and look down to see if the eye of your elbow is tracking with your thumb.
10. Continue to breathe wide to the side and into your ribs, and relax your jaw.

11. Reach your left hand up above your left shoulder to where it is comfortable. Firm your left arm and your left shoulder blade on your back.
12. Imagine you are creating width through your collarbones, as if you could reach your left fingertips a little higher while still grounded down into the right hand.
13. Lengthen your spine, reaching through the crown of your head.
14. Keep your neck in a long line with your spine. Tone the front of your throat with an energetic connection between your chin and your chest.
15. To come out of the pose, bring your left foot in front of you for support and then lower your pelvis down to the floor.

TEACHING NOTES ON SIDE PLANK

Side Plank helps to strengthen the hands and shoulders while preparing students for poses like Crow and Handstand. Start with new students by having them lift up into Side Plank and take a few breaths and then come down to rest. At first, whatever muscles are dominant in their patterns of movement will be overused in the pose. Some students will try to muscle through the pose while focusing on their shoulders. Others may recruit their back muscles to stabilize the pose rather than their core. This is a whole-body pose, and we want to remind students to engage not just the shoulders and back, but also the thighs, glutes, and abdominals. Watch for shoulder blade stability with this pose. Can the students keep their shoulder blades firmly on their backs, or do they begin to sink down?

If the student is letting their weight-bearing shoulder move towards their ear or dropping their pelvis down toward the mat, then they may need to modify the pose at first. These students need to work on gaining strength, so have them place a foot on the mat in front of them. In other words, if they are balancing on their right hand, then have them bend their left knee and place their left foot on the mat in front. Another option that will make the pose even more accessible for older beginners or those recovering from injuries is to have them start on their side, resting on their right hip and forearm with both knees bent, one stacked on the other, in line with their hips. When they press into their forearms and lift up their pelvis, their lower legs are then behind them.

Long holds in Side Plank too soon can cause students to go into familiar patterns of using the large surface muscles without learning to access and recruit the deeper muscles of the inner core. Strength building poses like Side Plank require organization, integration, and awareness before extending the number of breaths practiced.

Awareness + Patience + Practice

What we would like to impart to our students about their hands, wrists, and elbows is a message of self-care: awareness + patience + practice = self-care. No matter what their daily living and work activities entail, they will benefit from becoming aware of how they feel. When students are starting a yoga practice, we can help guide them to start slowly, pay attention, and back off when necessary. With patience and practice, we can all learn to do less at first. There is always "next time" to do a little more.

10
REALIGNING THE NECK AND HEAD

As we've discussed in previous chapters, many of our students will arrive at class with some degree of a forward head posture. Recently, I was waiting for a friend near the local campus and began watching to see how many misaligned shoulders and necks I could find. There were so many that I lost count! Age didn't matter. Students, professors, and staff all spend a lot of time on their phones and computers, and it is slowly affecting the posture of everyone who is not actively working to counteract it. This forward head posture puts a huge amount of pressure on the cervical vertebrae and muscles, especially at the C6-C7 level[1]; the further forward our head moves, the more dramatically the pressure and weight increases on the neck. In many cases, the shoulders are also rolled forward, and the neck and head follow the shoulders. As we continue looking at our devices all day, the head ends up stuck in this forward position. Over time it can lead to neck pain, headaches, and even surgery.[2]

How far forward the head rests, and the effect on the cervical spine depends on a number of factors, including the type of device we are using, the total screen time, and whether we need bifocals. For those of us who work on a computer all day not only is our head forward of our shoulders, but also sometimes the cervical spine ends up in a deep extension, especially at the top. Meanwhile, our face moves forward towards the computer screen, taking the shoulders with it. After I sit at my computer too long, I can feel my posture suffering, and in my mind I have this funny image of my face actually being sucked into my computer screen! This situation is worse with the use of laptops, as it is hard to keep good posture when the keyboard and screen are so close together. If a person uses bifocals to read their screen, then they will often make the cervical spine extension worse by jutting their chin forward in order to read the text through the bottom of their lenses. Forward head posture manifests differently with those who spend a great deal of time on their phones. They develop a type of forward head posture that has been dubbed "text neck." In this case, the cervical spine is straightened as the person looks down at their phone for hours a day.

ALIGNING THE HEAD ON TOP OF THE NECK

The good news is that a gentle and consistent yoga practice can begin to correct misalignments. The first step is to help students become aware of their neck and head position. Many times when students with forward head posture see a picture of themselves from the side view they are shocked, because they had no idea their neck was sticking out like that. The first thing they often do is try to send their chin and jaw straight back. The problem with forcing the chin straight back is that it creates tension with the muscles at top of the cervical spine and doesn't really fix the problem long term.

There are three movements we need to help students understand to begin to correct this postural issue. The first is one we've talked about throughout this book is learning to elongate the spine all the way up through the top of the cervical vertebrae. The second is to widen through the collar bones and begin to bring the shoulder blades onto the back (discussed in Chapter 8). Finally, in this chapter we need to address how the skull is positioned on the neck, and this is often the hardest movement fundamental to teach.

One place to start with educating students is to ask them to nod their heads up and down as if to say "yes" and ask them if they feel how their skull rocks on the top of their necks like the legs of a rocking chair forward and backward.

Practice: Aligning the Head on Top of the Neck

1. Standing in Mountain, elongate your spine from the bottom to the top, imaging you are reaching the crown of your head upward.
2. Move your chin down towards your chest and feel the back of the upper neck stretching out. Place your fingers on your upper neck and notice how the area becomes very firm the closer your chin comes to your chest. This is a deep flexion of the upper cervical.
3. Now, lift your chin upward and feel the compression occurring at the very top of the cervical spine and base of the skull. Again, place your fingers at the base of your skull, and feel how the bones of the upper cervical spine and the skull have come together. This is a deep extension of the upper neck.
4. Slowly nod your head up and down as if saying "yes," and see if you can feel the path the skull is following as it "rocks" on the top of your spine.
5. Find a neutral position for your head that is somewhere in between the extension and flexion.
6. Elongate your spine again and imagine that your head is floating right above your neck like a balloon[3]

After students come into awareness of their alignment issues, we can work with them to open the chest, strengthen the upper back, tone the muscles at the front of the throat, and elongate the spine all the way through from bottom to top. We can also educate our students about better posture throughout their day at their computers and phones. If they use bifocals, then suggest they invest in a pair of computer/reading glasses so they do not have to lift their chin up to read. When researching standing desks and special furniture to assist students in solving their pain issues, I also found companies that specialize in more posture-friendly keyboards and mouse devices.[4]

One great place to start with guiding students into positional awareness of the neck is the standing poses. The forward head posture often creates a challenge in just turning the head to the side with good alignment.

HAPPY NECKS IN SIDE ANGLE AND TRIANGLE

With the common alignment issues mentioned above, it is not always comfortable or even possible for these students to turn the head completely to one side in the standing poses. In an attempt to look like the teacher or the pictures they have seen of Triangle, students will try to crank their heads around to look up at the ceiling or at their hands. Often in the process of forcing the twist, the student will take the neck into extension, jutting the chin out and then turning the head. In other cases when a student finds they cannot turn their head in a neutral position they will take the neck into flexion and then turn the head. Both of these workarounds create discomfort in the neck and shoulders, and they can make cervical issues worse. By cueing different options for the shoulders and head position, we can give students ways for creating more comfort while they are still working on regaining the natural curve of their cervical spine.

When we see these common misalignments in Side Angle and Triangle, we can offer the option of looking at a wall across the room instead of trying to rotate and look up at the ceiling. If we keep our gaze in a direction similar to where the sternum is facing, then we can focus on lengthening the neck first, keeping it in line with the spine, and then perhaps rotating a little more as is comfortable. If students struggle to keep their neck in line with the spine, or if the neck is uncomfortable, then another option is to have them look down towards the floor in these postures. Although the option to look down is often flagged as "wrong alignment" by some teachers, it is actually a strong position for supporting the cervical spine, with a better energetic connection to the muscles of the upper back.

Newer students will also sometimes lift their heads up to level their eyes in these postures. It is a natural reaction to always want to level the head and eyes, especially for people who haven't done a lot of movement classes. This puts pressure on the side of the cervical spine and also creates pinching and discomfort. If verbal cues don't work to address this, then I stand in the pose right in front of the student and move my neck side to side asking them to follow my movement. I stop moving when my neck is right in line with the rest of my spine. When the student "gets it" that they were lifting up their head, it often elicits a giggle, in part because I probably look pretty silly bobbing my head around.

For those with known serious neck issues, these postures may not be appropriate at all due to the pressure the weight of the head places on the neck. Remember that our heads weigh at least 10 pounds or more, so holding it out to the side for any length of time takes strength in the neck and shoulder muscles.

WORKING ON TURNING THE HEAD IN WARRIOR 2

In Warrior 2, one option is to suggest students place their hands and arms a little forward of the body. The hands and arms are traditionally placed directly over the legs. This is visually pleasing, but for those who come in with posture issues, it creates tension at the back of the shoulders and into the neck. We are designed to do our work using our hands and arms in front of our body, so it is natural for the hands and arms to drift forward in the postures. If the hands are a little forward of the legs in the pose, then the head doesn't have to turn to an extreme range of motion in order to look over the fingertips. In this gentler approach, the body can open up slowly and students can work gradually towards the traditional version of the hands and arms over the legs if they desire. In the end, what matters is how they feel in the posture, not how they look in it.

Beginner version of Warrior 2 that is especially helpful for those students with posture issues. Hands are above shoulder height and are also slightly in front of the body.

Practice: Warrior 2

1. Start in Mountain while facing the long side of your mat. Then from Mountain, take a comfortable, wide stance.
2. Pivot on your left heel as you laterally rotate your left hip. Let your knees and toes follow so they are pointing towards the front of your mat.
3. Let your right hip remain in a neutral position with your knee and toes pointing towards the side of your mat. Or if it is available to you, pivot on your right heel and gently rotate

your right hip medially with your big toe mound planted slightly forward of your heel.

4. Place your heels in a line or a little wider.
5. Ground into your big toe mounds and outer heels and bend your left knee. Bend your knee enough to feel your left thigh working, but not so much that your knees or hips are uncomfortable.
6. Press your legs away from each other as if you are trying to make your mat a little longer; feel your thighs and glutes firming.
7. Imagine you are zipping up your belly from pubic bone to belly button.
8. Stretch your arms out into a T position with the hands slightly higher than the shoulders. Let your hands be slightly forward of your shoulders if that feels better.
9. Let your hips stay where they have naturally ended up. As you tone your low belly towards the left, gently rotate your ribs to the right. Again, let your arms float to a position where your shoulders are comfortable.
10. Bring your hands behind your head and clasp your fingers, letting your elbows be in a comfortable position.
11. Supporting your head with your hands, imagine that a string is attached to your skull just above your pinky fingers and it is gently drawing up the back of your head, like an antenna on a radio being pulled up.
12. Gently press your hands into your head and your head into your hands. Feel the muscles on the front of your throat firming.
13. Keeping the tone at the front of your throat, release your hands and stretch your arms back out to your Warrior 2 position.
14. Gently turn your head towards your left hand and bend your left knee a little more to deepen the pose. Feel your breath coming in and out of your ribs.
15. To come out of the pose, ground firmly into your feet as you

straighten your left leg. Pivot on your left heel, and then step back into Mountain.

AWARENESS OF THE CHIN/CHEST CONNECTION

As we've been discussing, our neck is designed to go in many directions so that we can quickly observe what is going on around us. Together, our eyes and head follow whatever we are focused on. In our everyday life, we look side to side and up and down, but if we stay in one position too long, our necks and shoulders start to hurt. This is true with yoga poses too. If we always keep the neck in the exact same position in a pose, then it may not be serving us over time. When we look at the yoga magazines from the 80s and 90s, many of the common postures included looking at the hands with the neck in deep extension. For instance, in Warrior 1 a typical instruction was to look directly up at the hands and let the neck drop way back for a dramatic effect. Another example is Warrior 3, where students were cued to lift up the head and look past the hands across the room. Teachers and students came to the realization that putting the neck into extension all the time in these postures was creating neck pain and injuries. Although the constant looking at the hands in the Warrior poses has fallen out of favor with many of the leading teachers, it's still very popular in some versions of the Sun Salutations. Students will lift their arms at the beginning of the Sun Salutation and then look up through their hands to the ceiling and then leave the neck in extension as they swan dive forward. Although we do need this range of motion available to us, repeating this over and over again causes neck issues for some students. In addition, when we drop our necks back, even if it doesn't seem to hurt, we lose the connection to our core.

Although the core/neck connection doesn't make sense to some at first, with practice we learn that all the bandhas connect and work together. The Jalandhara Bandha at the throat connects energetically with Uddiyana Bandha in the belly, and Mula Bandha at the pelvic floor.[5] So when we let our neck drop backward into a deep extension without any tone at the front of the throat, we are not as integrated with our core. Take a moment to notice what happens to your chest when you lift up your chin and let your head drop backwards. The chest drops subtly as the front of the throat loses tone. If we tone the muscles at the front of the throat while keeping an energetic connection between our chin and chest, the chest will lift a little, and it will be easier to keep our deep belly toned. Some yogis can learn over time to keep their throat toned while their neck is in extension, such as a deep Camel. For beginners, if we cue them to keep that energetic connection between the chin and chest, then they will find and access their whole core more quickly.

Cueing this subtle fundamental is a challenge, and changing up our language as we are working with a group can be helpful. Suggesting that students interlace their fingers behind their heads as we did above in Warrior 2 is one option. Other popular cues I've heard all have merit, but with each one some students misunderstand or overdo it. One example is telling students to "tuck the chin." It works for some, but others just let their chin drop and don't understand what we are doing. One of my Pilates teachers expressed frustration with a popular cue she had learned: "imagine you are holding an orange under your chin." Although some students understood that she wanted them to tone their throat, she laughed and said, "they all seemed to imagine a different sized orange!" In the singing world, teachers also want this healthy alignment as it opens up the soft palate and improves the quality of the sound. One of our studio teachers, Anne Roberts, is also a professional singer, and she likes to say, "smile at the back of your throat." Once a student learns to understand imagery, it's worth trying anything you can think up to see if you can help them find this connection.

For visual learners who are having trouble with this whole concept, it can help to have them take their right hand and curl their three middle fingers in. Then place their thumb on the middle of their sternum and their stretched-out pinky just under the tip of the chin.

Explain to them that this is a neutral position for the head, and you are asking them to not let their chin lift up off their pinky. Keep in mind that people have different sized hands and necks, and so you may need to give feedback on the exact hand placement with some individuals.

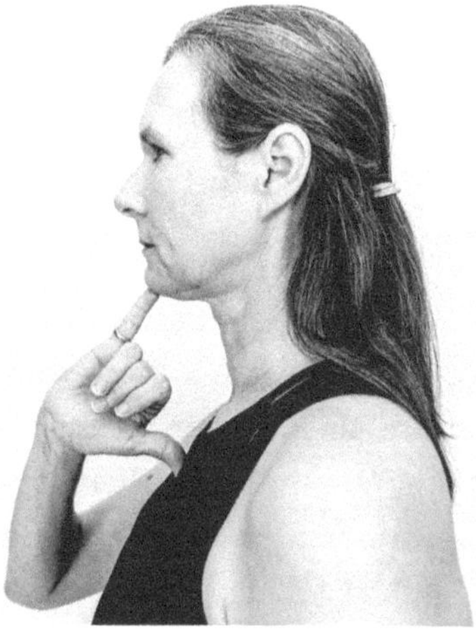

Placing the thumb on the chest and the pinky on the chin is helpful for visual learners who have trouble with the concept of the Chin/Chest Connection.

KEEPING THE CHIN/CHEST CONNECTION IN CAMEL

When I first tried Camel, I didn't like it at all because it hurt my neck. There was pinching and pain at the back of my neck, and I felt like I was straining at the front of my throat. The problem was twofold: the muscles at the front of my throat lacked tone and strength, and I was dropping my head too far back to try to look like the pictures I had seen in yoga books. Now, when I practice Camel, I keep my neck in line with my spine and choose not to drop my head back or lift my chin. Instead, I focus on lifting up my chest, toning my throat, and taking my shoulders back. One of my teacher friends can lift her chin, open her chest, drop her head back some, and still clearly keep her throat toned. It doesn't hurt her at all, and she looks beautiful in it. Each of us needs to experiment until we discover what works for us.

Practice: Camel

1. From Table come upright onto your knees and place a block on its highest level near the outside of each ankle.
2. Bring your knees and lower legs below the hips or a little wider.
3. Lengthen your spine as you reach through the crown of your head. Feel your breath coming in and out of your ribs.
4. Soften the fronts of your hips by folding forward a little for a moment, and then straighten yourself again, bringing your pelvis into a neutral position.
5. Work your legs apart gently as if you had a resistance band around your thighs.
6. Wrap your hip pointers towards each other while toning your low belly. On your back, imagine you are lifting your sacrum up towards the base of your skull.
7. To prevent dropping your head back too far, curl your middle three fingers on your right hand and then place your right thumb on the middle of your sternum and your right pinky just under your chin. To focus on toning the front of your throat, imagine that you are lifting the top of your sternum towards the top and back of your neck at C1.
8. While staying firm and stable below the waist and keeping your pelvis over your knees, begin to lift your chest up to create a backbend in your upper back (thoracic spine). Imagine a string is attached to the chest and is lifting the chest upward.
9. As your chest lifts, let your gaze lift with it, still keeping the connection you established between the chin and the chest.
10. Reach your fingertips back on both sides and find the blocks. Press your fingertips into the blocks and lift your chest up a

little more if available to you. If you can't reach the blocks, then place your hands on the back of your pelvis.

11. To come out of the pose, first bow your head forward, then firm your thighs as you move your hands to your hips to come up.
12. Rest for a few breaths in Pose of the Child.

Teaching Tips for Camel

Students with a wider pelvis often complain about their lower backs hurting in this pose. For these students, we can try placing their knees a little wider than the traditional hip-distance apart. The narrower stance causes some of these students to start in too deep of an anterior pelvic tilt. When they widen their stance, they can let the sacrum drop down and better connect with the glutes to stabilize the pelvis. Focusing on imagery to engage the deep transverse abdominals and all the muscles that work with them also helps to stabilize the pelvis and the sacrum.

Beginners, attempting to get their hands on their heels will hinge backwards from their knees and work their thighs. Moving our thighs back and forth while on the knees is not a bad exercise in itself (it's called Thigh Stretch in Pilates), but in this yoga pose we are focusing on a backbend, not a thigh exercise. One way to help convey this concept is to take students to the wall and have everyone place their thighs as close to the wall as they can without anything hurting. Blankets can be placed under the knees for those who need the support. Ask them to place their hands on the wall at about shoulder height and press the hands and fingertips into the wall while isometrically drawing them downwards. This drawing down of the hands will help students feel the muscles of the upper back firming as the backbend moves more into their upper back and not just the lumbar spine. Another cue to help encourage a little more movement in the upper back is to imagine a string attached to the chest and lifting the chest upward.

TEACHING INVERSIONS WITH CHIN/CHEST CONNECTION

It is better in mixed level classes to focus on inversion preparations and strengthening exercises rather than full inversions, as it is hard to guide everyone safely in this situation. *Students must have a healthy posture before attempting inversions.* If the "deskansana" and forward head posture are not addressed first, then students will increase the risk of injuring themselves. For students who are ready for full inversions, then I teach them in private sessions or smaller groups.

In the beginning, is it easiest for many students to first learn Headstand preparation. Learning to hold an inverted tucked position with the knees at the chest helps students learn abdominal control and stability. By wrapping the hands around the head and pressing the head into the hands, we firm the front of the throat and the back of the neck and upper back are also very engaged. Headstand is more stable than Forearm Stand or Handstand, in part because of the active chin/chest connection created by the hands pressing into the back of the head.

The tucked position in Headstand helps the student learn to get control and stability in the torso and hips before straightening the legs. Taking a moment to have students hold the tucked position, firm up their thighs and buttocks, and then send the legs up makes a huge difference for beginners. Working towards just stepping into the tucked positions rather than kicking or rocking into it is the best practice. This way the students will learn to get into Headstand with total control.

There is a safety issue for the neck in Headstand that is often overlooked when teachers feel pressured to introduce inversions. Too much pressure on the top of the head puts an immense amount of pressure onto the neck, and the cervical spine is not designed to hold the weight of our bodies. Although there are yogis who can easily hold this pose for 10 minutes or more and not hurt themselves, this is not something that should be attempted by new students. Most of the weight needs to be in the forearms and elbows with just a little weight on the top of the head.

Students who first start by learning to hold an inverted tucked position often have greater abdominal control and stability when they later attempt the full Headstand.

Options for the Neck in Forearm Stand and Handstand

When I first learned to do Handstand, I was taught the traditional way: look at a point on the floor to steady the gaze and then kick up. Focusing on a point helps with orientation and balance while upside down. Over the years, kicking up has become less popular, and some teachers are now suggesting students step up into a tucked position first with control as we discussed above with Headstand. This takes time and a lot of work to master, but there are two reasons I think it is a great option. The first is stability. Just as in Headstand, the core is required to hold the tucked position. I've seen many students make little progress towards Handstand as they wildly kick up to the wall, often coming into a backbend with little core engagement. The second reason I find the tuck more effective is that students can work on looking across the room in this more stable position, keeping the chin/chest connection while inverted. After teaching students that toning the front of the throat helps us stay connected with our core and pelvic floor, then it seems logical to apply this same fundamental to inversions. For most people though, when they are first learning inversions it's too scary to not look down at the floor. The focus on the floor helps with orientation and alleviates the fear of flipping all the way over. However, it is worth encouraging students to work towards this, because in the long run their poses will be more stable and integrated.

Placing the feet on the wall or a chair for the "L" Handstand is a great way to build strength and focus on fundamentals.

To give students an idea of what it feels like to have the front of the throat toned in Handstand, we can start them first with a traditional handstand preparation that goes back many years in yoga: the "L" position at the wall.

Practice: "L" Handstand at the Wall

1. Place your mat with one of the short sides against a wall and get a strap.
2. To find proper hand placement for this pose, first sit with your back against the wall and your knees bent.
3. Place a yoga strap under the soles of your feet and then stretch your legs out in front of you into Staff, letting the strap move with your feet. Once in Staff, the strap should be lying on your mat right at your feet, and this marks where to place your hands for this practice.
4. Leaving the strap where it is, transition to your hands and knees and place the heels of your hands just in front of the strap.
5. Press evenly into your whole hands, including the heels, the knuckle pads, and the fingertips.
6. Draw your belly in and up, and keep your knees bent, curl your toes under and lift your pelvis up into Downward Dog. The heels of your feet may rest on the wall.
7. Imagine you are gently hugging your forearms towards each other as you tone your biceps and underarms.
8. Move your right foot a little to the center, shift your torso forward some, and then lift your left foot and place the mounds of your left toes on the wall at hip height.
9. Press strongly into your left foot and straighten your left leg as you bring your right foot up to hip height onto the wall. You are now in an upside down "L" shaped handstand.
10. Continue to lift your belly in and up as you breathe into your ribs.
11. Bring your attention to your neck. Rather than looking at your hands let your neck be long and in line with your spine. Feel an energetic connection between your chin and your

chest, toning the front of your throat. If you struggle to connect with your throat while upside down, then try to imagine something more concrete, like you are holding a large orange under your chin.

12. To come out of the pose, keep your core engaged, bend your knees some, and bring one foot and then the other to the floor. Come down onto your knees and visit Pose of the Child to breathe and rest.

BUILDING STRENGTH AND AWARENESS BEFORE INVERSIONS

When I first started taking yoga classes many years ago inversions were not taught in beginning classes. Instead, we worked on inversion preparations like the "L" Handstand practice above. Even when I traveled around the country and toured studios at that time, I only saw inversions in classes marked intermediate or advanced. There was often a progression of classes that students were required to attend, much the way martial arts studios take students through levels. Due to the explosion of yoga, yoga trainings, and yoga classes, the market has changed to something much more competitive, and the culture in classes has also changed significantly. Some new students see the pictures on social media of yogis doing inversions, and they come to classes wanting to learn handstands. Attempts to hold this type of student back until they learn to get connected with the core and shoulders often end with them leaving for another studio. At the same time, some teachers who like doing handstands themselves include them in all their classes without first teaching the basics of alignment and preparatory poses to build the proper strength. Sometimes, students feel pressured to attempt handstand when that is not why they came to yoga. The result of all this is that many people don't progress into holding their handstands, but just continually try to kick up, and get frustrated. Some of them hurt their wrists and shoulders, and some just get bored of it, since they can't ever "stick" the handstand.

Giving new students the option of doing something else while teaching inversions doesn't always work, as certain personalities will try it anyway. Some adult students think they are still 16 years old and do not have a realistic idea of what state their body is in. Do you have a friend who is out of shape but still goes to the gym a few times a month? Does that friend also tell you how they want to go and try out for the American Ninja Warrior TV show when it comes to the metro near you? This is the friend who comes to yoga class and wants to do handstands on the first day. To reduce injuries in yoga, we need to provide better preparation and also insist that beginners keep their feet on the floor until their posture is healthy and they reach a specific set of milestones.

There are four milestones that I want students to achieve before teaching them inversions.

1. Strong Core and Pelvic Stability: Students must be able to hold a forearm plank with good form for at least 1 minute. Specifically, good form means their shoulder blades are completely firm on their backs. They are not rounding their upper back, nor letting their chest drop down. The pelvis is in line with the whole body, not dropping down below or lifting up above the shoulders. Can they hold their pelvis in a neutral position in this posture?
2. Shoulder Range of Motion (ROM): Can they easily take their arms directly over their head and support the weight of their upper body without bending their elbows? Observe the student in Downward Dog: Does their head come easily between their arms? Is there a long line from their wrists all the way up to their hips?
3. Shoulder Blade Stability and Positional Awareness. This is also tested with the core test above. Watch to make sure their shoulder blades do not move around on their back in forearm plank, and that the medial side of the shoulder blade does not pop up like a chicken wing. In addition, see if they can hold a

side plank with their shoulder blades stable for at least 30 seconds. For positional awareness, watch them as they do the Dolphin elevation/depression exercise (last practice in Chapter 8). Can they hold their shoulder blades in a neutral or a slightly elevated position? Can they feel the difference of what position their blades are in when they are upside down in Dolphin?

4. Supple Hamstrings: If their hamstrings are too tight then they won't be able to walk their feet close enough to their elbows or hands to get their pelvis up over their shoulders for inversions. Trying to kick up with the feet too far from the hands creates instability. See if the student can lift one leg up in Downward Dog for a Three-Legged Dog and then start to walk their hands back towards their feet.

LIFTING C6/C7 IN SHOULDERSTAND AND PLOW

It is hard to get any real data as to how many people hurt their necks in Shoulderstand, but anecdotally I believe that it happens more than most yoga teachers would like to admit. Students often complain about their necks after trying this pose, and there has always been a lot of chatter in yoga circles about the possibility of injuries and strokes when the pose is held too long.[6] Originally, the teaching was to bring your chin as close to the chest as possible to create an extremely deep flexion in the neck. We've learned that this puts a great deal of pressure on the bottom of the cervical spine at C6/C7.

One of the best ways to avoid issues is to place a stack of blankets under the shoulders, to reduce the flexion of the neck. Even though using blankets in Shoulderstand and Plow has been taught in yoga for years, there are still yogis that refuse to use them for a variety of reasons. For me, blankets are a safety net. If I lose the integrity of the pose by not focusing for a moment or by just losing strength, then the blanket is there to ensure that I don't end up putting weight on the back of my neck. Pressing the elbows into the blankets and then hugging them towards each other gently works the upper back muscles to lift up the C6/C7 area. One reason students don't like blankets is that sometimes they just don't feel as secure; they feel like their elbows slip out to the side on the blankets, or that the blankets move around underneath them. I went through this at first, but once I got used to the blankets, I did notice that my neck wasn't as sore, and now I prefer using them. A possible solution during the learning phase is to add another mat on top of the blankets, even wrapping the mat around one side of the blanket stack to create a feeling of stability. Mats can also be placed between the blankets.

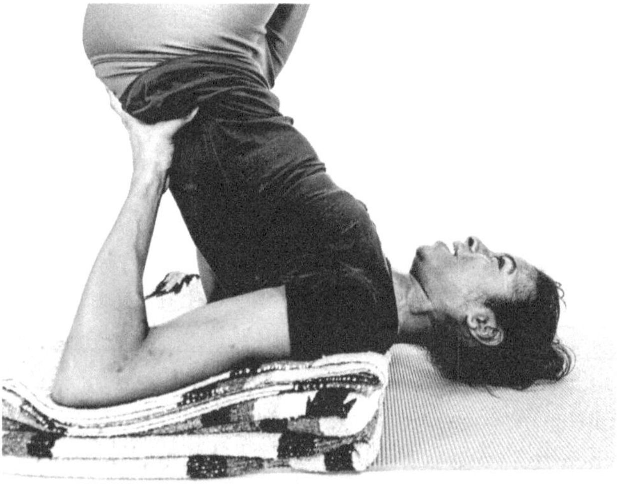

For the safety of the neck, align blankets with the top of the shoulders so that the C6/C7 area is floating off the edge of the blankets and there is no weight directly on the neck.

Most gyms do not provide yoga blankets due the cost of purchasing them and keeping them clean. This presents a particularly difficult situation for yoga teachers when students want to learn Shoulderstand and Plow at the gym. Avoiding these poses in the venues where there are no props is the best practice, especially with mixed level groups that include beginners. There are many ways of making the class "hard" without taking people into poses that they are not ready for yet. Focus on poses at first with the head inverted like 3-Legged

Downward Dog and Dolphin to help students gain experience and strength. If the situation is such that avoiding the pose is difficult, then modify Shoulderstand by asking students not to go past their shoulder blades, keeping them at more of an angle, hinged at the hips, with their hands on the back of the pelvis and the feet over their heads.

This modified version of Shoulderstand is safer at the gym where blankets are usually not available.

Practice: Supported Shoulder Stand

1. Fold your yoga blankets fringe to fringe, and then fringe to fringe again, and then finally fold the fringe side to the side with no fringe. This leaves the blankets neatly folded with all the fringe to one side and a smooth folded edge on the other. We call this "Tadasana of the Blanket."[7]

2. Stack at least 2 or more blankets with the smooth folded edges even in the middle of your mat.
3. Lie down on your back on the blankets with the top of your shoulders in line with the smooth folded edges of the blankets.
4. Make sure your neck, including the very bottom of your neck at C6/C7 is floating off the edge of the folds of the blanket, and the back of your head is on the mat.
5. Bring your knees in towards your chest and lift up your pelvis, getting your hands under your pelvis to help support you.
6. Keep your elbows about shoulder-width apart and press them down into the blankets and gently towards each other, creating a lifting feeling through the chest.
7. Keeping the hands on the back of the pelvis for support, begin to straighten your legs toward the ceiling as best that you can to create a V shape with your body at first.
8. Tone the low belly by zipping up from pubic bone to belly button and wrapping the hip pointers towards each other.
9. Keeping the abdominals firm, begin to lift the pelvis higher and let it shift forward towards your shoulders.
10. Adjust your hands, moving them towards the top of your pelvis near your waist, and lower back as you lift up into Shoulderstand.
11. Breathe evenly into the ribs while keeping your belly toned.
12. Firm your legs and press the sides of the big toe mounds into each other.
13. If bringing the feet together feels too narrow, then bring them hip-distance apart and work to activate the feet and calves along with toning the thighs and lifting up the glutes.
14. Keep gently hugging your elbows in and activating the lift of the chest and C6/C7.
15. When you begin to struggle with keeping the feeling of lifting up through C6/C7, then it is time to come out of the pose. Bring your knees to your chest first, and then your hands to the floor to support you as you come down out of the pose.

TIPS FOR AVOIDING NECK INJURIES

As students begin to work towards a healthier cervical alignment, they may also experience soreness and tightness in the neck. In an attempt to stretch it out, they try the classic neck roll as seen in many exercise classes including yoga. However, while rolling the neck around in a circle may seem like a relaxing way to loosen up, it may actually create new problems and aggravate current ones. Unlike the ball and socket joint of the hip, which can rotate in a circle, the cervical spine is designed to move quickly in different directions with our gaze. Students may aggravate disc problems and/or muscles that are tight or weak with this rolling move. Older students with osteoporosis are at risk for damaging their vertebra. A safer and more effective movement is to take the neck in one direction, to the side for instance, and then come back to center before moving in the next direction. Another way to add neck stretches into class, when students are on their backs or stomachs, is to have them turn the head from one side to the other, stopping and breathing on each side.

Skip the Chin Stands

Another popular set of moves seen on social media and advertising are the chin stands or balances. In these inversions, the chin is resting on the mat and is stretched out in front of the yogi as they kick up their legs into a balance. Although the hands, shoulders, and chest are supposed to be taking the majority of the weight, the chin is part of the tripod of support. I have yoga friends who love doing these, and they appear to be able to do it without hurting themselves. Like any rule we make in movement, someone is going to be able to break the rule and remain unscathed. However, these chin stands are something that I will not practice myself and I won't teach them. The possibilities of damaging my own cervical spine or one of my students is just too high, and we need our necks for the rest of our lives. Even if the teacher does a great job and talks about lifting the body up and away from the chin, powerfully using the back muscles to create space, the possibilities of the body weight dumping forward onto the chin are too great a risk in my opinion. Putting weight onto the neck, especially when it's in a deep extension, can cause disc problems and perhaps worse. It's not a pose to be showing to beginners or teaching to those who are yoga weekend warriors. Leave these postures for the acrobats who train three or more hours a day for these postures and tricks. Acrobatic yoga teachers, with years of experience, who know how to sequence for these types of tricks, along with how to properly spot, should be sought out before attempting these poses.

Awareness + Asana + Alignment

In summary, the forward head posture is a modern-day crisis that we must help our students understand for the sake of their long-term health. First, they need to become aware of how they are holding their head and neck, and second they need to learn how to safely and effectively come into alignment. Once students find the chin/chest connection, the core becomes more integrated within all the poses. Through creative cueing, we can help bring the body back into a healthy alignment, with a focus on how students feel rather than how they look in the poses.

11

SHAVASANA: THE RELAXATION POSE

When I ask new teacher trainees about their Shavasana experiences, I hear a variety of stories, as teachers lead Shavasana in many different ways. Sometimes a poem, quote, or guided relaxation is read, and other times music is played. Although there are variations in the way Shavasana is taught, the main focus is learning to relax the body. It is a practice of "undoing" and learning to stop and be present.

Learning to relax and breathe is not only practiced in Shavasana, but also in yoga nidra, restorative yoga, and meditation. Even though these practices overlap, they also have specific differences. In yoga nidra, the teacher, sometimes with a script, guides students into a resting state called yogic sleep. When practicing restorative yoga, students relax while supported in different reclined positions in silence. Finally, meditation is an active practice of listening and watching our own thoughts. When we teach Shavasana, students may experience aspects of these other practices organically. For example, once a student learns to let go and relax in Shavasana, they begin to notice their thoughts, and this can be the beginning of learning to meditate. No matter what students experience, our main focus when teaching Shavasana is to offer them time to relax, breathe, and be present.

WHY IS SHAVASANA SO IMPORTANT IN TODAY'S CULTURE?

Our culture does not do relaxation well. We are all about working hard and not wasting any time. Constant input from our electronic devices in the form of news and entertainment also keep us from taking time to reflect. Some of us are caught in the cycle of always keeping up with what is going on with pop culture and our groups on social media. Afraid we will miss something important, we resist unplugging from our digital world. We stay busy and often feel frustrated that we cannot finish everything, and so we live in a dysfunctional relationship with time.

All the pressure to work, keep up, succeed, and have the perfect life that we see represented on social media creates stress, health issues, and often a chaotic inner world. By guiding students through Shavasana, we are hoping to teach them that relaxation is a life skill. It's good for us, and it's ok to stop working sometimes. Taking care of ourselves, resting, and doing yoga is not a waste of time. In fact, it's a great investment of time because when we do learn to practice Shavasana and relax, our bodies begin to heal themselves.

When we learn to rest and reflect, our mind quiets and answers begin to bubble up about our life's dreams, callings, problems, and relationships. Regardless of our background or personal beliefs, many of us who have discovered yoga agree that we have experienced some kind of spiritual connection in Shavasana. Practicing regularly creates a groundedness from which we can better deal with life's day-to-day challenges and transforms our inner world into one of love, acceptance, and compassion for ourselves and others.

Educating the Resistance

Shavasana is the hardest pose for many students to learn, because as we discussed above, they think it is a waste of time. I call this "the Resistance." Students also resist the practice of Shavasana for a variety of other reasons, including not seeing self-care as important (but they always care for others), becoming aware of physical pain, memories and triggers from trauma, and mental health issues including anxiety and depression.

As more mental health practitioners have joined the practice, we have learned that some of the traditional ways teachers have dealt with the Resistance are often not effective and may do unintended harm. Some examples of these teaching practices include requiring students to close their eyes, remain completely still, remain in one specific position, practice in darkness, and remain in class by locking the door. We now know that these strict requirements may make Shavasana more difficult for some students to learn due to experiences of physical or mental trauma in their lives.[1] Being still and quieting the mind may bring up difficult memories and emotions, and so we must not force students to try this pose. It must be an invitation. We can accept that there will be resistance for a variety of reasons, and work with kindness and gentleness to create a culture in our classes that is supportive of learning Shavasana over time.

I meet people where they are in terms of their readiness for Shavasana. For the overachieving personality, I tell them that Shavasana is an advanced pose that takes most students a while to understand. This appeals to their ego, as they want to be advanced and so they lie down immediately and try to do it better than everyone else. There is some humor in this, but it's the first step in learning the pose for them. For other students, including those who appear unsure or confused, I offer different options to try and put them at ease. We will go over these options below. Before and after class, I talk about Shavasana often with students, about my own experiences, and why I like it so much. This lets them know that it is something that is important to me. Even if they don't want to lie down at the end of class, they might do it anyway just to please the teacher. The group dynamic is also very helpful. If a few students really get Shavasana and enjoy it, then others will follow along to be part of the group.

When a student gets up to leave early and disrupts Shavasana by rolling up their mat and getting out their keys, my choice has been to just ignore it in the moment, and try to speak to the student alone later. I always allow students to leave before Shavasana if they don't want to do it, but I ask them to please do so well before we lie down so that they don't interrupt others who are trying to learn the practice. This usually works to stop the interruptions, and the conversation often leads to the student trying Shavasana the next time. Once we get to know the students, we may be able to ask them why they are leaving early, and if there is anything they need to be more comfortable. Sometimes when I've had trouble getting a group to accept Shavasana, I've relied on what worked the best for me as a mother: positive reinforcement. At the end of class, when the students that stayed sit up, I make a positive statement about how great it was that they chose to stay for Shavasana, the hardest pose.

TEACHING SHAVASANA TO MIXED LEVEL GROUPS

No matter where we teach, we can offer students many options for "setting up" for Shavasana. These options help to create an easy-going atmosphere where most students will feel comfortable and choose to participate. Although lying down flat on the back is the tradition, we can offer students any position that is comfortable for them, such as lying on their side, lying on their side with their back against a wall, lying on their stomach, sitting upright, or sitting as they rest their back against the wall. Those with back issues such as scoliosis may prefer lying on their stomach or side. The objective is to encourage students to stop, relax, and breathe, and so if they need to start in one of these alternative positions then we should encourage this. As they choose what position is best for them, let students know that it is OK once Shavasana begins to move around quietly in order to get comfortable, to get a drink if they are coughing, or even to just sit up to finish if needed. No matter what position students choose, we can offer padding or support with blankets and/or bolsters if available.

For those who are lordotic (sway back/extension issues), Shavasana will be more comfortable if they put their legs over a bolster, over a foam roller, or onto a chair. These students will complain that their low back pinches or hurts and will keep bringing up their knees and putting their feet flat on the mat to alleviate the discomfort. Other students will experience neck discomfort, rooted in their forward head posture, and try to put something under their head. We can guide them to put just enough support under their head with a gym towel or yoga blanket to be comfortable, and to prevent their chin from sticking up higher than their forehead. Too much height under the head reinforces the forward head posture, and it is better to encourage them to lie as flat as is comfortable in order to let gravity do the work of opening their chest and bringing their neck into alignment.

Many new teachers struggle with what approach to take when teaching Shavasana. How long should it be? What should be said? There is not just one right way to guide people into relaxation, and for each yoga group, we may need to try different approaches until something works. For my hour and fifteen-minute classes, I encourage the experienced students to practice Shavasana for 10 minutes or more in silence with no music or distractions. With beginners, however, this is often too long, especially if the class is only 50 or 60 minutes. Starting with five minutes or less and playing some soft background music is a nice start. When I use music for this purpose, I will often turn the music down towards the end of Shavasana so that students experience at least a minute of silence. Over time, they may learn to like the silence, and students may even ask for the music to be turned off.

Some Options for Leading Shavasana:

1. Lead a guided awareness, starting from the head and moving down the body towards the feet. Example: "Feel the breath coming in and out. Notice your face and jaw. Feel your shoulders supported by the floor…."
2. Read an inspiring quote or poem to the group, and then play soft music for a few minutes.
3. Read a guided imagery passage. For example: "Imagine that you are at a sunny beach. Hear the sound of the waves, and feel the warm sand supporting you." We must know the class first in order to pick an appropriate passage for this option.
4. Lead a pranayama practice, such as Viloma, to help them relax into Shavasana (see discussion below).

Depending on where we teach, we may have to change our plans for Shavasana in order to be effective. In the gym environment, we often have to play music to drown out noises from other classrooms or the weight room. The use of guided relaxations, if we have a microphone, can be helpful to keep students focused in this often-distracting environment. In the studio environment, we have the option of using bolsters and blankets, and this allows us to sometimes end our classes with a restorative yoga pose. Restorative yoga, which has been popularized by yoga teacher Judith Lasater,[2] consists of resting in a pose with the body fully supported by props like bolsters and blankets. Once students accept the basic Shavasana, introducing them to this deeper practice of restorative yoga is incredibly rewarding for teacher and student.

No matter what options we choose when teaching, we will need to proceed with patience. Some students have an experience in which they appreciate Shavasana quickly, while others take many years to catch on. One yoga teacher friend of mine told me that it took her three years to like Shavasana. She just kept lying down because everyone else was and she wanted to be part of the group, but due to her personal issues at the time, she just wasn't open to experiencing the resting pose. Slowly, class after class after class, Shavasana worked on her, and one day she realized that she had been enjoying the pose. The energy of the group helps to carry those through the practice who may need support. We go farther together than we do alone.

STARTING SHAVASANA WITH PRANAYAMA

Pranayama is often described as breath control or breath exercises. I experience it more like communing with my breath. Whenever we try to talk about a spiritual experience, words fail us, and so the word "commune" is the best I can find to explain how it feels to me. Communing means communicating with each other, or experiencing life, at an intimate level. Essentially, I make it a habit to "hang out" with my breath like I'm with my best friends from college. When I go to my college reunion, I find myself in the flow of real connection with a group of people who know me better than anyone else. They already know what is broken about me, and they don't care. They support me, they listen, and I listen and support them. It's a similar feeling of intensity and intimacy that we can find listening, watching, and communing with our breath. Pranayama to me is much like walking in the ocean along the shoreline. We have no control over the waves, but we can be present and centered within the life force and energy of the water.

There are many types of pranayama that are practiced in different ways depending on the style of yoga. Some pranayama techniques are meant to increase or balance energy, while others help us to relax. The ones that help us relax and calm our mind can become a bridge to both Shavasana and meditation. The techniques help us to focus on our breathing, which then reduces the chatter in our minds. Once the mind begins to quiet, we can cease the pranayama practice as we drop into Shavasana.

One of my favorite pranayama practices for starting Shavasana is Viloma because it is not only relaxing but also simple to teach. There are variations of Viloma, but the one I start students with is an adapted version, beginning on the inhalation. Viloma means "against the natural flow of the breath," and in this practice, we stop the natural flow of the breath. With Viloma on the inhale, we begin to inhale and then pause for a moment, and then continue inhaling, and then pause for a moment again, and so on, usually adding 3 to 5 pauses. This traditional pausing of the breath can sometimes cause tension for beginners, as they may focus too much on holding the breath, and it can also create anxiety. Another option that often works for beginners is to cue a little exhale of the breath during the pause to reduce tension. For example, we begin inhaling, and then we pause to release a little exhale, and then begin inhaling again. When students are ready to practice more intensely, we can offer the traditional version of imagining that we are breathing up a set of stairs, stopping to pause at each step.[3] In mixed level classes that include beginners, the best practice is to start slowly and offer options, because breath practices, like Shavasana, can bring up uncomfortable feelings and experiences. The stillness and focus on the breath in pranayama may make symptoms worse for students who are suffering from depression and anxiety.

Practice: Beginning Viloma on the Inhalation

1. Lie on your back with your feet flat and your knees up. If needed, place a bolster under your knees for comfort. Another option is to place a bolster or rolled up blanket under your back and along your spine to open up your chest.
2. After you settle in and get comfortable, bring your attention to your breath.
3. Soften your belly and take a small, natural, relaxed inhale, and then exhale a little.
4. Now inhale more into your ribs, then exhale a little.
5. Next, finish your inhalation as you breathe into your chest, pause for a moment, and then exhale a long, smooth breath.
6. After a few rounds practicing steps 3 through 5, try counting

to 4 on the inhales and to 2 on the exhales. If you begin to relax into this practice, then you can try counting a little higher until you discover the best pace for yourself.

Relax + Let Go + Let Be

After spending hours in teacher training talking about alignment and anatomy of the postures, sometimes I joke around and say, "all that stuff was just to wear you out so that we can teach you Shavasana!" Even though I am trying to lighten the mood with the remark, I believe this is true. Shavasana is the most important thing we can teach our students. As I wrote in the introduction, many students come and go from our classes, and in the limited time they are present we want to teach them what is most important. Whether they are able to do Downward Dog correctly doesn't matter so much, as it is unlikely they will continue doing it anyway. If they learn Shavasana, however, then it may have a lasting ripple effect throughout their lives and the lives of their family and friends. It has the potential for so much positive change that we must teach Shavasana every time we teach yoga, even when there are only a few students and they seem uninterested.

Many years ago my brother, a musician, gave me some great advice when I complained to him about the challenges of running a studio. He said, "Always play like you are playing for a full house." Always teach yoga to the best of your ability, as you never know who might be there that day and finally "get it."

NOTES

1. GUIDING BREATH AWARENESS

1. Nancy Zi, *The Art of Breathing: Six Simple Lessons to Improve Performance, Health, and Well-Being.* (Glendale: Vivi Company, 2000), p. 12.
2. Leon Chaitow, Dinah Bradley, Christopher Gilbert, *Recognizing and Treating Breathing Disorders: A Multidisciplinary Approach,* Ed. 2. (Edinbough: Elsevier Ltd., 2014).
3. Donna Fahri, *The Breathing Book,* (New York: Owl Books, 1996) EPUB, p. 772.
4. Blandine Calais-Germain, *Anatomy of Movement* Rev.ed. (Seattle: Eastland Press, 2007), p. 62.
5. Erich Schiffman, *The Spirit and Practice of Moving into Stillness,* (New York: Pocket Books, 1996), p. 54.
6. The work of slowly moving through the spine vertebra by vertebra was not a huge part of yoga, with the exception perhaps of dvipada pitham (breathing bridge), depending on how it was taught. Working through the spine, vertebra by vertebra like a wave, was a major part of Joseph Pilates' teaching in the 1930s and 1940s. This exercise may have been partly popularized by him.
7. Anne M.R. Agur, Arthur F. Dalley II, *Grant's Atlas of Anatomy* Rev. Ed. 13. (Baltimore: Lippincott Williams & Wilkins, 2013), p. 37.

2. OPENING AND GROUNDING THE FEET

1. Variations of fancy toe yoga were popularized by Aadil Palkhivala, from Purna Yoga College in Bellevue, WA, starting in the late 1990's and then by the hundreds of yoga teachers who have studied with him. No matter what variations you have learned or want to create yourself, just go slowly, as these exercises can be very frustrating to new students.
2. Mark Singleton, *Yoga Body: The Origins of Modern Posture Practice,* (New York: Oxford University Press, 2010), p. 180.
3. Anne M.R. Agur, Arthur F. Dalley, *Grant's Atlas of Anatomy, 13th Edition,* (Baltimore: Lippincott Williams & Wilkins, 2013), p. 415. The angle between the femur and the tibia is referred to clinically as the Q-Angle, and it is generally greater in women due to their wider hips.

3. ALIGNING THE FEET AND ANKLES WITH THE KNEES

1. I was also influenced by my conversations a few years ago with Sierra Codalata, an OU dance student. Her teachers, including Austin Hartel, encouraged their students to teach turnout from the hips.
2. Bernie Clark, *Your Body, Your Yoga: Learn Alignment Cues That are Skillful, Safe and Best Suited to You*, (Vancouver: Wild Strawberry Productions, 2016.), p. 239. See this reference for a deeper understanding of the anatomy and ROM differences of the ankle.
3. Less commonly it goes to the adductor attachments on the front leg as the student attempts to square the hips while also keeping the front knee over the ankle. This will create pain at the inner knee or at the groin.

4. ACTIVATING THE QUADRICEPS AND GLUTES

1. This pattern is known as Lower Crossed Syndrome, a term originated by Dr. Vladimir Janda and now actively used by physical therapists, yoga therapists, and Pilates teachers. For a description of his work and how to apply it to yoga postures, see: Doug Keller, *The Therapeutic Wisdom of Yoga*, Vol. 1: Foundations, (Sterling, VA: DoYoga Productions, 2018), p.57.
2. MacAskill, Durant, Wallace, "Gluteal muscle activity during weight bearing and non-weight bearing exercise." *International Journal Sports Physical Therapy*, 2014 Dec; 9(7):907-14.

5. STRETCHING THE HIPS CAREFULLY

1. Blandine Calais-Germain, *Anatomy of Movement* Rev. Ed., (Seattle: Eastland Press, Inc., 2007), p. 205.
2. The labrum of the hip is a fibrocartilaginous ring around the edge of the hip socket that helps to keep the head of the femur in place. For a description of this common injury, see, "Hip Labral Tear", Mayo Clinic online, www.mayoclinic.org/diseases-conditions/hip-labral-tear/symptoms-causes/syc-20354873.
3. Kathryn L. Havens, Susan M. Sigward, (2015). "Cutting mechanics: relation to performance and anterior cruciate ligament injury risk." The journal of Medical Science Sports Exercise, 818-24; Apr;47(4).
4. Doug Keller, *The Therapeutic Wisdom of Yoga*, Vol. 2 Applications, (South Riding, VA 2018), p.68.
5. One source for more information about how a tight pelvic floor affects the hips: Eric Franklin, *Pelvic Power, Mind/Body Exercises for Strength, Flexibility, Posture, and Balance*, (Hightstown, NJ: Princeton Book Company 2002), p.38.
6. Doug Keller introduced this idea of floating the heels in forward bends.

6. AWAKENING THE CORE AND STABILIZING THE PELVIS

1. Nora St. John, *Balanced Body Pilates Instructor Training Manual, Mat 1,* (Sacramento: Balanced Body, Inc., 2010), p.57.
2. Michael Freeman, Mark Woodham, Andrew Woodham, (2010). "The Role of the Lumbar Multifidus in Chronic Low Back Pain: A Review." PM & R: The Journal of *Injury, Function, and Rehabilitation,* 2. 142-6; 10.1016/j.pmrj.2009.11.006.
3. The zipper imagery is credited to Lulu Sweigard, a student of Mable Elsworth Todd. It has been popularized over the last 20 years by Doug Keller and Eric Franklin. Our use of it involves drawing the low belly together towards the midline while lifting upward and activating the deeper abdominals. However, Sweigard's work involved imagery only, as the dancers she trained would imagine various images while lying still to improve skeletal alignment over time.
4. Blandine Calais-Germain, *The Female Pelvis: Anatomy and Exercises,* (Seattle: Eastland Press, Inc., 2003), p. 30-31.
5. B.K.S. Iyengar, *Light on Yoga,* (New York: Schocken Books, 1966), p. 246-248.

7. FREEING THE SPINE

1. Michael Schuenke, Erik Schultz, Udo Schumacher, *Thieme Atlas of Anatomy, General Anatomy and Musculoskeletal System,* (New York: Thieme 2006), p.100-101.
2. Vanda Scarevelli, *Awakening the Spine,* (NewYork: Harper Collins Publishers, 1991), p. 31.
3. Dowels around 4 feet long and 1/2 inch in diameter work well for this.
4. Thanks to the Bergamo retreat teachers who are always brilliant and helpful. In the 1920's the pose included a variation with the chest on the floor and the arms also at ninety degrees. This wasn't accessible to most students, and so for this and historical reasons, the pose fell out of favor. Yoga teachers have made it more accessible over the years and renamed it.

8. STABILIZING THE SHOULDERS AND OPENING THE CHEST

1. Santa Fe yogi Sean Tebor introduced me to using these shorter dowels in my yoga practice many years ago.
2. Blandine Calais-Germain, *Anatomy of Movement* Rev. Ed., (Seattle: Eastland Press, 2007), p.121.

9. SUPPORTING THE WRISTS, HANDS, AND ELBOWS

1. Anne M.R. Agur, Arthur F. Dalley, *Grant's Atlas of Anatomy*, 13th Ed., (Baltimore: Lippincott Williams &Wilkins, 2003) p. 564.
2. Erhan Yilmaz, Lokman Karakurt, Oktay Belhan, Mehmet Bulut, Erhan Serin, Mustafa Avci, "Variation of carrying angle with age, sex, and special reference to side.," *Orthopedics* (Nov 2005): 1360-3.
3. Michael Schuenke, Erik Schultz, Udo Schumacher, *Thieme Atlas of Anatomy*, (Stuttgart, Germany: Georg Thieme Verlag, 2006) p.244. The carrying angle represents the angle between the humerus and the ulna and is determined by the shape of the humeral trochlea.
4. As a mother, I give any other parent or friend of a child with a large carrying angle permission to copy this section of my book and gently give it to the coach.
5. Eric Franklin, *Dynamic Alignment Through Imagery*, 2nd Ed. (Human Kinetics: UK, 2012) Chapter 5, Fig. 5.2. Balloon imagery here inspired by Mabel Elsworth Todd and Lulu Sweigard.

10. REALIGNING THE NECK AND HEAD

1. Erik Dalton, *Advanced Myoskeletal Techniques*, (Oklahoma City: Freedom From Pain Institute, www.erikdalton.com, 2010), p. 233.
2. Kenneth K. Hansraj, MD, "Assessment of Stresses in the Cervical Spine Caused by Posture and Position of the Head." *Surgical Technology International, 2014* Nov;25:277-9.
3. Lulu E. Sweigard, *Human Movement Potential*, (Allegro Editions, 1974) p. 249. Her imagery, including the balloon referenced here, was inspired by the work of Mabel Elsworth Todd and popularized in the last 20 years by Eric Franklin.
4. https://www.kinesis-ergo.com.
5. Through slow and continued awareness work, we can begin to pulse our pelvic floor and feel the bounce or pulse in our soft palate at the back or our throat.
6. William J. Broad, *The Science of Yoga: The Risks and the Rewards*, (New York: Simon and Schuster Paperbacks, 2012).
7. Judith Hanson Lasater coined the term "Tadasana of the blanket" with her restorative yoga teachings.

11. SHAVASANA: THE RELAXATION POSE

1. Bessel Van Der Kolk, M.D., *The Body Keeps the Score: Brain, Mind, and Body in the Healing of Trauma*, (New York, NY: Penguin Books, 2014), p.273
2. Judith Lasater, *Relax and Renew: Restful Yoga for Stressful Times*, (Berkely, CA: Rodmell Press, 1995).
3. Swami Niranjanananda Saraswati, *Prana and Pranayama*, (Munger, Bihar, India: Yoga Publications Trust, 2016), 180.

PRACTICE INDEX

Below you'll find a listing of all the practices in this book grouped by type. In the ebook edition the link will take you to the nearest subheading so you can easily find the practice.

BREATHING AND PRANAYAMA

STANDING

ON HANDS/FOREARMS AND FEET

SEATED

BACKBENDS

- Pigeon (Ch 5)
- Modified Pigeon on the Back with a Big Car Wash Sponge (Ch 5)
- Locust (Ch 7)
- Upward Dog (Ch 9)
- Camel (Ch 10)

TWISTS

- Teaching Abdominal Awareness in Twisting (Ch 7)
- Sage Twist (Ch 1)
- Rotating the Ribcage Subtly with the Breath (Ch 7)
- Revolved Pinwheel with Alternate Side Breathing (Ch 7)

CORE WORK

- Finding the Bony Landmarks of the Pelvis (Ch 6)
- Opposite Arm Leg Balance (Bird Dog) (Ch 6)
- Pelvic Tilts with a Big Car Wash Sponge (Ch 6)
- Side-Lying Flow with Sleeping Vishnu (Ch 6)

SHOULDER WORK

- Protraction/Retraction and Elevation/Depression of the Shoulder Blades (Ch 8)
- Foam Roller Shoulder Warm-up and Chest Opener (Ch 8)
- Shoulder Stretches with a Dowel (Ch 8)

INVERSIONS

- "L" Handstand at the Wall (Ch 10)
- Supported Shoulder Stand (Ch 10)

EXTRAS

- Fancy Toe Yoga (Ch 2)
- Alignment of the Head on Top of the Neck (Ch 10)

ACKNOWLEDGMENTS

Over the last few years while writing this book, I was also running a yoga studio. If you imagine what it might be like to run a yoga studio, then you will not be surprised that I have a lot of people to thank! I'm a big picture and big idea person, and not the best at details. So the completion of this book was dependent on a lot of people helping me with class lists, accounting, phone calls, toilet paper and paper towels, teacher trainings, and our online offerings. During the pandemic in 2020, I decided not to renew the lease on the studio. After 15 years I closed the brick and mortar and began to focus full time on our online offerings and my writing projects.

Our last studio manager, Kelly Phillips, led us all with positivity and professionalism. She is one of the most organized people I've ever met, and this book would not have been completed without her. I started seriously writing it in 2017 when my friend Holly Jack was our studio manager. At that time, I was struggling with burnout and the demands of being a studio owner. Holly took over. She ran the studio herself for about a year while I rested and got back into my own practice. I'd also like to thank Leanna Boyd, our first studio manager, who continues to call me and rally me to finish this book.

Kathie Hibbs, Tim Bodenstein, and Jeri Smalley have been instrumental in developing and teaching our trainings, allowing me more time for writing and other projects. Kathie is the kind of person you can always count on, Tim keeps everyone on an even keel with his chill yogi vibes, and Jeri makes sure every detail is correct. I also want to thank the teachers and staff who have served our students over the last few years, including Melissa Hearn, Lisa Millington, Tiffany Nguyen, Barb Pyle, Anne Roberts, Aimee Rook, and Lauren Schueler.

Over the years, I've taken classes and workshops from many yoga and pilates teachers, and I've learned something from each one of them. Early on I was introduced to yoga by Martita Stearns, and mentored as a young teacher by Maggie Metzinger, Shannon Caldwell White, and Diane Jackson. Through the workshops that Diane hosted at that time, I met Doug Keller in 2003. Doug quickly became by favorite teacher, and he helped me immensely with my teaching and the curriculum for my 200-hour program. My teaching and writing continues to be influenced by Doug's work, and I cannot thank him enough for his time and mentorship over the years.

I've learned so much from my editor, Angela Nicolosi, over the last 2 years. I feel like I'm a better teacher and writer after working with her. Angela became my anchor person for this project and has seen it to the end, which is a huge gift to me. Angela brings a certain grounded, steady energy to her work along with a loving heart. I'd also like to thank Emily Smith and Leann Nequette for reading the manuscript early on and providing feedback and support.

We had a lot of fun working on the photographs. Alix Yaw became part of the creative team right away and worked hard to capture what I had envisioned. Kelly, Tim, and Holly were joined by Jenae James to pose for the photographs. Jenae has been a positive force in my life for many years, and I appreciate her support on this project.

Before publishing this book I reached out to my yoga friends asking them if they would read an advanced copy and provide feedback. I was overwhelmed by the response and support I received. To everyone who read even part of the book, thank you so much. I'd especially like to thank Heather Clark Hilliard, Anne Roberts, Jeri Smalley, and Ellen Wisdom for their time and feedback on the entire manuscript.

Through the years of stopping and starting this book project, my family has always been supportive. My parents have encouraged me to do good work and make a contribution with whatever I did. Kirsten, our youngest, also loves to write, and during their college years we would meet at coffee shops and write together. While sitting and thinking about what I wanted to write, I could hear the keys on Kirsten's computer tapping away, the youthful energy and enthusiasm emanating in all directions. Our oldest, Carolyn, seems to have inherited the organizing gene from someone other than me, and over the last year has been a huge help with the studio and the manuscript. Many years ago I said I wanted to write a book, and my husband Randy has patiently encouraged and supported me through the process. Writing a book is a long, hard process, and knowing that he believed in me made a huge difference in completing the project.

Finally, I would like to thank the students who have come to Yogalife over the years. The students teach me more than I teach them. For their presence and support I am truly grateful.

-Becca Hewes, June 2021

ABOUT THE EDITOR

Angela Nicolosi, C-IAYT, ERYT500

Angela Nicolosi has over 35 years of experience as a yoga therapist and teacher. She draws on her background in dance, clinical mental health, chronic pain management, and iRest yoga nidra to provide both private yoga therapy and group classes. Her areas of specialty include chronic pain, illness, and neurological conditions. Currently she is focused on applying yoga therapy practices with clients who have ALS and cognitive challenges.

ABOUT THE AUTHOR

Becca Hewes, C-IAYT, ERYT500

Becca Hewes, a yoga teacher and teacher trainer, fuses classic yoga with Pilates exercises to improve her students' movement patterns, core integration, and strength. After owning a neighborhood studio for 15 years in Norman, Oklahoma, she is now offering her classes and popular RYT200 training online at Yogalife.tv. Becca is certified as a Yoga Therapist through the International Association of Yoga Therapists (C-IAYT) and is registered at the highest level with Yoga Alliance (ERYT500). *Teaching Yoga* is Becca's first book.

Yogalife.tv

facebook.com/yogalifetv

VIDEOS INCLUDED

We've been working on videos to go with this book!
Sign-up on our site and we will send you a link to access the free *Teaching Yoga* video collection.

yogalife.tv/getvideos

In addition, you'll get more information about the continuing education courses we are producing based on this book and other topics.

You can also take live online classes with Becca at Yogalife.tv.